The Prostate Chronicles:
A Medical Memoir

By Bob Tierno

Mind Over Bladder Publishing

2019

© Bob Tierno and "Mind Over Bladder Publishing" 2019
ISBN 9781095160015

All rights reserved. No portion of this book may be reproduced in any form without permission from the author, except for brief excerpts for reviews.

Cover design by VikNCharlie at Fiverr

First Edition

To **Karen**, who has been an integral part of my life for over 50 years. A saint by some accounts (it's true), and in this fight for the long haul (with her own detour the same day as my surgery).

To my parents, **Rocky and Carm Tierno,** for without them I wouldn't be here. Rocky was my hero, a Pearl Harbor Survivor, West Point graduate class of 1949, wounded in Korea and served our country for thirty three years, retiring as a Colonel. He even commanded a military group in Bolivia in the 1970's. Carmela, "Mom T," was an Army officers wife, a true force of nature. She was a world class chef and taught us the enjoyment of international food. Unfortunately, she had a long struggle with Alzheimer's and passed away fourteen months after Rocky. They are both resting peacefully at the U.S. Military Academy at West Point.

To **Dale (deceased) and Floretta Jones,** Karen's parents who trusted me with their daughter. I'll be forever grateful for their support.

In addition, I am dedicating this book to spouses, family, friends, business associates, fraternity brothers, and neighbors like Tom and Jan Knox and Linda Smith, who were there for us in our time of need.

This book is also dedicated to all of the men out there who unwittingly became members of an elite club with an initiation ritual of a diagnosis of prostate cancer.

To **Jon Obermeyer** for his book *Big Splash: Writing Your First Book*. He was the writing coach extraordinaire with a six month plan keeping me on point. Thanks!

My gratitude to My Lord and Savior Jesus Christ, St. Joseph, St. Francis of Assisi, St. Christopher and The Virgin Mary, for watching over me.

Circumstance does not make the man; it reveals him to himself.
- James Allen, As a Man Thinketh

Life is either a daring adventure or nothing at all.
- Helen Keller

I left a trail of footprints deep in the snow
I swore one day I would retrace them
But when I turned around I found
That the wind had erased them.
- Dan Fogelberg, "The Last Nail"

23. Prostate Popsicles (Cryotherapy, Cryoablation)
24. Radiation and Brachytherapy: Keep Your Powder Dry
25. What me MRI?
26. A Radical Course
27. "Houston We Have a Problem" (Karen Takes Flight)

Section IV: The Post-Game Show
28. Post-Op.
29. Post-Surgery Diet: You Are What You Eat
30. Surgery Results
31. Mind Over Bladder
32. Pickleball Redemption
33. Building Your Army of Support
34. Financial Planning: Get Your House in Order

Section V. Survivor Stories
35. Survivors
36. "Terry Talk"
37. "Ray and the Robot"
38. Tomba
39. Dennis: Don't Rely on the Biopsy
40. My Cousin
41. TK
42. The Other Bob: Two Decades Cancer-Free
43. Is There an Author in the House?
44. Chris from Shanghai

Postscript
The Curtain Rod - A Point of Clarity
Gratitude

Appendix

Contents

Foreword: Dr. Richard Bevan-Thomas M.D.
Introduction

Section I: Teeing Up the Ball
1. Life is a Book, Made Up of Chapters
2. Turning 70 - Taking Stock
3. Dynamic Cynicism

Section II: The Prostate Conversation
4. The Prostate: The Gland That Brought You to the Dance
5. Prostate Cancer - Stat.
6. The Andy Grove Effect
7. The Love/Hate Relationship with your Urologist
8. Misery Loves Company: Give me a Break!
9. Locating Your Libido (It's Not Where You Think)

Section III. The Detour
10. Diagnosis
11. Face your Fear, Face Your Foley Catheter
12. The Gleason Score Roulette Wheel
13. This is Your New Life
14. Treatment Scenarios: They All Suck
15. Elevated PSA but no Cancer
16. Hormone Therapy
17. Do Nothing (and Die)
18. Homeopathic Medicine
19. Functional Medicine
20. Naturopathic Medicine
21. Watchful Waiting
22. Active Surveillance

Foreword

When Bob told me he was writing a book on prostate cancer during a recent appointment at my clinic, I paused for a minute. I prepared myself for another "Invasion of the Prostate Snatchers" book. Then he asked me to write the foreword for the book. This was definitely getting awkward.

Fortunately, Bob continued on about why he wrote the book and how he was a contributor to several online prostate cancer forums. My interest piqued and after reading the book, I agreed to write this foreword.

Bob has written a memoir of his prostate cancer experience that I think many readers will enjoy.

Bob's witty comments like "your mileage may vary" and his reference to "life's runway" brings in his sense of humor of how he handled his diagnosis of prostate cancer.

Men handle this challenging diagnosis differently but it is refreshing to hear that despite taking his diagnosis seriously, Bob was able to reflect at length in "The Prostate Chronicles." He provides several good recommendations for men diagnosed with prostate cancer.

As a Urologist specializing in robotic surgery, I encourage my patients to use social networking for support. While most men rely on support from their immediate family, having support from other men who have experienced the same diagnosis can never be underestimated.

There are multiple challenges that men face with a new prostate cancer diagnosis. The most important recommendation that I give patients is, "don't panic."

I recommend patients perform their due diligence in finding the best Urologist and Radiation Oncologist to discuss options and make sure to ask the tough questions. Is a prostate MRI advised? Is genetic testing an option?

I advise patients and families to start at the beginning and understand their cancer and where they are on the spectrum of the disease process.

With a dose of humor and many prostate cancer facts, Bob's journey is a raw and unbiased approach to addressing prostate cancer. I hope men find this memoir useful.

Richard Bevan-Thomas, M.D.
Urologist & Prostate Cancer Specialist
Urology Partners of North Texas

Introduction

I know not all that may be coming, but be it will, I'll go laughing.
- Herman Melville, *Moby Dick*

Frankly, most books on prostate cancer are boring and predictable, with an over-emphasis on the medical aspect. This book is irreverent and therefore it is different. It sheds a light on a personal journey and speaks to how relationships matter.

Men generally don't like to speak about their prostate because of its impact on their ego (sex life) and quality of life (incontinence).

Life as they knew it is "over", not acknowledging that their life already sucked thanks to their prostate. As in always asking for an aisle seat near the restroom. As in always looking for the nearest bathroom at events, and of course, not enjoying that favorite cup of joe if a bathroom was more than an hour away.

You do have a number of options when diagnosed with prostate cancer, but frankly, they all suck. Despite numerous downside implications, there is the ultimate outcome that you live to see another 10, 15 or 20 years. Having that definitive end-of-life conversation with my urologist was sobering to say the least.

Whether you are a husband or a significant other, prostate cancer is a steady part of our health lexicon today. If you are lucky enough to live to age 80, you will most likely face it.

I think of prostate cancer as a detour in my life in my late 60's, something I would not have asked for and something that had no A-Z manual.

If you happen to have prostate cancer, you're not totally FUBAR (Fouled up beyond all repair) Ok, maybe a just little bit. At least you won't ever again have to hear your urologist say BOHICA, Bend Over Here it Comes Again!

Ella Wheeler said in her famous poem "Solitude,"[1]: "laugh and the whole world laughs with you. Weep and you weep alone."

Prostate cancer sucks, but you stand a better chance coping if you have humor on your side. I'm choosing to take a humorous approach because:

a) it's freaking healthy,
b) why not?
c) because I can.

Frankly, I don't see many options when faced with a cancer that can kill me (worst case), or make my daily life miserable even with proper treatment.

Imagine having to change your incontinence underwear multiple times a day (while at work, or tailgating before the game), Worse yet, having your penis shriveled up like a mushroom cap, never to be rock hard again. Adios, date night!

And in my case, as a diehard Oklahoma Sooner, who wouldn't laugh about an ultrasound rod inserted into my rectal orifice by a Texas Aggie urologist who's also a drilling for cancerous cores on the other side of my rectal wall like he's looking for the next Spindletop?

Now let's move onto the Comedy Zone known as surgery. Here's a laugh.

I imitated a side of beef, hung by my ankles to allow a robot to drill six incisions in my abdomen, extract my cancerous prostate, seminal vesicles, detach my urethra from my bladder, then reattach it inserting a long straw through my penis to allow the bladder to drain for 24 hours.

Now, let's finish the party with a suprapubic catheter (external) piped into the bladder below my navel.

Every single bit of this was conducted by a surgeon on a XBox Game Boy called da Vinci, which replaced old school radical surgery guttting me like a 12 point elk being dressed out following the hunt. Imagine surgical repair by a robot. "I'll be back".....The Terminator.

My life has been a series of exciting eras, all of them fueled by my love of experiencing new challenges. I'm knowledgeable about a lot of things, to which I can now add prostate cancer and robotic surgery. Not my first choice, but it does make the list of my expertise longer.

As a former sailboat owner, I learned quickly to focus on the horizon or I would get seasick. In my lifetime I have lived in over thirty-one homes, including apartments and a fraternity house.

My hero Jimmy Buffett sings about searching for that One Particular Harbor. In 2018, we were caught in a very large squall that almost sent us to Davy Jones Locker.

I wrote this book as an irreverent medical memoir.

Why?

In 2018, I was diagnosed with prostate cancer, one of the leading killers of men in our world. One in nine men (age 50-70) will be diagnosed with prostate cancer. 2 Most men will either die of something else or prostate cancer by the time they are 80. How's that for a future? Welcome to my world.

This book is about a major detour I took on my life's journey as I neared my 70th birthday. It's also about my wife's losing battle with a marble floor and dueling patients at home. More importantly I wrote it for other men as well.

I've organized this book focusing first on my life's experience, secondly on the importance of relationships (your spouse or significant other as your advocate). And finally, clear sailing ahead. It ends well, I can tell you

And that's my point, shining a light on your path, so you can get to where I am today: PSA <0.01, undetectable.

Lord knows we need to shine a bright light on prostate cancer; it's been in the dark far too long. That's the way a killer operates, when you don't acknowledge it or talk about it.

As men, we need to share approaches to potential treatment solutions while learning how to build an army of support along the way. Spouses and significant others: you are the critical advocate and partner in this fight.

You will learn how Karen, my wife of 46 years, didn't shy from this responsibility and helped lead me to the treatment option that made the most sense. How a neighbor named Tom shared his story and reference material mentoring me through the eye of the needle.

Prostate cancer is an inflection point in a man's life. Only when diagnosed did I finally admit that all the warning signs were there, but I didn't share them with my primary doctor or my urologist. I not only had my head in the sand, I had my head up my ass in denial.

As they say in the airport, "If you see something, say something." As a prostate cancer survivor, I'm compelled to speak up and it's going to take me an entire book o pull it off.

I'm not being a wise ass, here. In no way am I attempting to demean or diminish any man's experience with prostate cancer. Laughter ultimately pulled me through to the Other Side.

This book is for you, to help you figure out what is going to get you there, what is deep within you, and in the family and friends that surround you.

Section I
Teeing Up the Ball

1
Life is a Book, Made Up of Chapters

You were born with the ability to change someone's life
-Author Unknown

Improvise, Adapt, and Overcome
-Marine Corps Slogan

After a 9 ½ year career with the Federal Prison System a in the early 1980's, Bob Derby a former Navy fighter pilot- turned Intel Corporation marketing legend hired me as an automotive customer marketing engineer (CME).

"Engineer?" Really? He must have overlooked my B.S. in History and an MBA in Marketing. My military background probably helped or perhaps it was my federal prison service experience? As in Correctional Officer, Administrative Systems Manager, Paralegal, and Regional Administrator. I don't know but I am thankful.

Bob had various philosophies but one has stuck with me my entire working life. Bob explained that career assignments are generally 18-24 months in length and are "chapters" or "eras" in one's life.

As an Army Brat, it was easy for me to relate as my father had numerous assignments every 12-18 months. He called us "Gypsy Travelers" a handle Karen and I took on as we moved through our chapters of life.

On my first day on the job as a correctional officer at the then Federal Youth Center in Englewood, Colorado I was given a tour through the various units and happened upon a young man in the work/study release unit. I asked "why" was he here? His response has resonated with me my entire adult life.

"Everybody needs to be somewhere and my somewhere is here." Of course "how" he got to this somewhere is pretty comical. "I went to a bank and borrowed money without signing for it." So with that , my somewhere in 2018 is a place called prostate cancer.

This book is about a chapter in my life that I hadn't planned on.

Or, let's call it a detour, caused by a diagnosis of prostate cancer at the sage age of 69. But of course it's not all about me. My bride of 46 years Karen (KT) helped study this disease and was preparing to be my caregiver when she took a different detour the very same day I had surgery (see Chapter 27).

DISC Drive
Albert Camus the famous French philosopher, author, and journalist wrote "It all becomes a question of style."

My behavioral style is what's known as a DISC, based upon Marston's Theory 3 about behavior which states that we all communicate/behave with at least two characteristics.

In case you're wondering, DISC stands for Dominant, Influence, Steadiness, and Compliant.

D - In the wild kingdom, the eagle represents **Dominant**, leaving carnage in its wake. The D needs to win, competitive by walking all over you with combat boots. The D personality keeps on trucking. If you haven't surmised, we're very competitive.

I-Influential is represented by a peacock who wants to be liked. I'm an off- the-charts Dominant Influential. I want you to like me but if you don't I'll make you, and soon.

S- Steadiness is represented by a dove; not wanting to upset the applecart and offend anybody. Resisting change not in a overt way but quietly hiding in plain sight. Said another way, I am risk averse.

C-Compliant is represented by an owl, who requires rules, data, detail before attempting to move forward. Very analytical, risk averse: bankers, accountants, engineers, PGA golf professionals. (Yes, PGA golf professionals-Fore!)

The DISC Author
Writing a book is a difficult and complex undertaking. There is so much to share and it took this cathartic event to dig in and start documenting my experience, in part to help you and your spouse/significant other on your journey.

Look on Amazon and you'll find over 9,000 books on prostate cancer. Few of them approach the topic with straight talk, irony, and of course humor.

My inner Eagle wants to make sure the prostate conversation includes and demonstrates the power of prayer, support from friends and neighbors, and an inner resilience. Or put another way, "Mind over Bladder."

I read comments every day from men with prostate cancer and it's time to "out" this cancer. Whether you have been diagnosed with prostate cancer, are recovering from treatment, or have a friend or associate that's making this life detour, this book is meant to be a frank, albeit irreverent conversation to have with your spouse, significant others, children, caregivers, and doctors.

Welcome to my era. There's hope in it, and humor. Life is is like that.

2
On Turning 70 - Taking Stock

The French are true romantics. They feel the only difference between a man of forty and one of seventy is thirty years of experience.
--- Maurice Chevalier

Age is not measured by years. Nature does not equally distribute energy. Some people are born old and tired while others are going strong at seventy.
--Dorothy Thompson

Karen and I were watching the end of year reviews on television and those famous people who passed on in 2018. I told her that it made me feel older. Karen said it made her feel vulnerable.

We both experienced vulnerability in 2018. When I got asked about my date of birth and say "49" for the year. The young lady on the other end of the line ask naively, "1949?" No, 1849 of course!

She apologized but it got me thinking about looking back on 70 years. Then I remembered a Bible passage.
"As they made their escape, one angel commanded Lot to "look not behind thee" (singular "thee"). However, as Sodom and Gomorrah were destroyed with brimstone and fire from the Lord, Lot's wife looked back at the city, and she became "a pillar of salt." (Genesis 19-24)

That parable is so true. If I look back too long (70 years is a long time), my mind freezes on specific dates and times: rock and roll music, my late mother and father, Rocky and Carmela Tierno, ten presidents, JFK, Vietnam, The Civil Rights Movement, Watergate, and Woodstock. The last time the Cleveland Browns won a world championship was 1964 when I was 14.

In the Fall of 1967, I was admitted to Oklahoma University as a non-resident student with a 2.4 GPA back in the day when all your parents needed was to write a check and fog a mirror. I am definitely grateful since I started my senior year in high school with a stellar 1.8 GPA. Not exactly Ivy League material.

There was campus unrest due to the Kent State shootings by the Ohio National Guard. I served as an assistant to the Afro-American student association president from Bedford-Stuyvesant, NYC. We made an odd couple. Bill Moffitt had a huge afro, and I was an Army ROTC cadet.

In a rebellious move I took on the university and off campus retailers by opening the Student Services Grocery Store, in response to the high prices levied on students by off-campus stores. My fraternity brothers pitched in to help get this fledgeling business off the ground. Bill Nation was our CFOAccountant, and Fred Streb was our construction superintendent. Our pinmates Karen and Karleen helped with the initial ordering and stocking.

Then there was the two-year Army ROTC escape valve from the draft notice for dropping an Italian class which lowered my credit hours to "draft my ass" status.

I lost entire summers to Fort Benning, Georgia and Fort Sill, Oklahoma. The "summer of love" was the "summer of wasn't" for me. My Deke fraternity brothers recently reminded me of how turbulent those times were with the Vietnam War raging on.

We lost one of our own, Randy Morrison, who enlisted in the Navy to become a medical corpsman who'd pull his time in San Diego. He was shipped off to Vietnam with a Marine unit and lost his life saving others.

Brother Ron Sorter was a young second lieutenant deployed to South Vietnam and lost a leg. The saga of his injury and long journey back to Colorado will be forever embedded in our memories. It will also be the subject of my next book. Ron, thank you for your service and sacrifice.

So, how does a beautiful coed who was born in Stillwater, Oklahoma, raised in Oklahoma City, find a wretch like me? We met on a blind date in 1969. I was smitten, so she parted ways with her handsome beau to become my Deke sweetheart, ultimately eloping in 1972. We've been through trials and tribulations over 46 years of wedded "bliss". In the mid '80s a young Intel Folsom engineer told Karen that she was a saint for being married to me.

In 1972, I couldn't believe that such a beautiful woman had agreed to marry me! I'm no saint. By the grace of God, Dekes in spite of their bad boy reputations, always manage to marry up. Karen is in a league of her own. There is a special place in Heaven for her.

Ten years after graduating from OU, I decided that if I was to achieve my dream of working in private industry, I'd have to earn a Pepperdine MBA. This two-year sprint included a professor of statistics who had a "mad on " for everybody in the class. I enlisted the aid of a fellow student and we took the guy out for drinks (emphasis on drinks) and a bite to eat after class.

This came to be known as "The Rose Wine Methode" of passing the course. It worked and our entire class was grateful for the sacrifices (aka hangovers) we made for the greater good.

So, why look back at 70 years? Memories, oh those memories that's why. They fill me with gratitude to have been granted this terrific life. Sure, I'd like a do over or two but there's no turning back.

And that's why when I was diagnosed with prostate cancer there was no weeping or gnashing of teeth. Okay, maybe a WTF? Karen and I want to age with style. Not withered and dependent on others. We live with an overwhelming sense of gratitude as we move forward because I'm playing with house money now.

Approaching 70 for me was almost derailed by prostate cancer and yes, the mundane but important tasks of updating insurance, wills, and final instructions. One thing a diagnosis like this will do for you is bring clarity to your thoughts, deeds, and actions in all of your relationships.

Death is inevitable. My philosophy of life is that it has been a barrel of fun and challenges along the way. Finally, make no mistake about it, any diagnosis of cancer is a cathartic experience.

3
Dynamic Cynicism

Sarcasm: Helping the intelligent politely tolerate the obtuse for thousands of years.
Unknown Author

The most wasted of all days is one without laughter.
– E. E. Cummings

What twisted trait enables me to make this detour without ample servings of depression and anxiety? Dynamic Cynicism (DC).

The recipe is a strong dose of an optimistic outlook, a healthy dose of God's love, a beautiful loving wife, a strange sense of sarcastic humor mixed together and letting it age for 69 years. What emerges is DC!

Humor me, or rather, humor is me.

DC on reflection is sarcasm wrapped in sheep's clothing, questioning/commenting on the most trivial of life's events. DC is not meant to harpoon or hurt anybody. It's more like a kevlar vest that protects me.

If you don't have a sense of humor and you are gearing up for your first Gleason score, I suggest you go out and buy some yucks, and do it quickly.

I reflect on my journey with prostate cancer and give those around me with a healthy dose of DC to stare down this deadly disease with middle finger raised high. I proudly claim that I am fluent in Dynamic Cynicism.

The Cancer Treatment Centers of America (CTCA) [4] have published the benefits of laughter, in part, "The healing power of laughter for people living with cancer, it may seem strange to find humor when facing such serious issues. Yet, laughter may be helpful in ways you may not have realized or imagined".

Laughter may help you feel better about yourself and the world around you. Laughter may be a natural diversion. When you laugh, no other thought comes to mind. Laughing may also induce physical changes in the body. After laughing for only a few minutes, you may feel better for hours.

When used in addition to conventional cancer treatments, laughter therapy may help in the overall healing process.

According to some studies [5], laughter therapy may provide physical benefits, such as helping to:
* Enhance oxygen intake
* Stimulate the heart and lungs
* Relax muscles throughout the body
*Trigger the release of endorphins (the body's natural painkillers)

* Ease digestion/soothe stomach aches
* Relieve pain
* Balance blood pressure
* Improve mental functions (i.e., alertness, memory, creativity)

Laughter therapy may also help to:
* Improve overall attitude
* Reduce stress/tension
* Promote relaxation
* Improve sleep
* Enhance quality of life
* Strengthen social bonds and relationships
* Produce a general sense of well-being

Here's a joke for you:

Hank is lying in bed in the hospital, wearing an oxygen mask over his mouth and nose. A young student nurse appears to give him a partial sponge bath.

"Nurse," he mumbles from behind the mask, "are my testicles black?"

Embarrassed, the young nurse replies, "I don't know, Sir."

I'm only here to wash your upper body and feet."

He struggles to ask again,

"Nurse, please check for me. Are my testicles black?"

Concerned that he might elevate his blood pressure and heart rate from worrying about his testicles, she overcomes her embarrassment and pulls back the covers.

She raises his gown, holds his manhood in one hand and his testicles gently in the other.

She looks very closely and says,

"There's nothing wrong with them, Sir. They look fine."

The man slowly pulls off his oxygen mask, and says very slowly, "thank you very much. That was wonderful. Now listen to me very, very closely:

"Are - my - test - results - back....!"

(Unknown Source)

Drum roll please.

Section II

The Prostate Conversation

4
The Prostate (the Gland That Brought Me to the Dance)

Life without sex might be safer but it would be unbearably dull. It is the sex instinct which makes women seem beautiful, which they are once in a blue moon, and men seem wise and brave, which they never are at all. Throttle it, denaturalize it, take it away, and human existence would be reduced to the prosaic, laborious, boresome, imbecile level of life in an anthill.
-Henry Louis Mencken

The prostate is a muscular walnut shaped gland about an inch and a half long that sits directly under the bladder. It's main function is to produce part of the fluid for semen.

The urethra pipe runs directly through it so that men can get warning signs that something bad may be happening in their prostate. The prostate grows over time and sometime in your sixties or seventies it may grow to the size of a lemon. Sweet huh?

The prostate is not a totally useless organ and plays a role in a man's sexual and urinary health, The good news is men can live without a prostate if radical surgery is the treatment of choice. It's the nerve bundles around it that are important for erections. The remaining sphincter muscle, controlling urinary and bowel movements, is hopefully working or trainable via Kegel exercises. If not, there are surgical and non surgical solutions.

So let's clear the air about a few items. If only part of the prostate is removed it can grow back. Nothing in my research recommended partially removing the prostate.

While writing this book I learned from a fellow Pickleball player that his associate at work was being rushed into surgery to remove a portion of his prostate due the fact it was so enlarged (BPH) he was unable to urinate. I am not sure how this will work and it doesn't apply to a partially cancerous prostate.

If the prostate gland is completely removed, it's gone forever. Therein lies the untruth all men seem to think that their sexual life dies with the removal of their prostate.

What ends is the ability to procreate. If your surgeon successfully saves most if not all of the nerve bundles on either side of your prostate, you are still in the game. They saved 100% on the left side and 85% on the right during my operation.

These nerves are important to a man's sexual performance. Men can experience orgasm albeit "dry," which means no procreation, but at 70 who cares?

This mysterious gland is of no consequence to a man until starting in his forties then changes may start to occur which is why the PSA Test as well as the Digital Rectal Exam (DRE) are so important.

The prostate starts to grow and may develop BPH or enlarged prostate putting pressure on the urethra which is why answering questions about urination frequency are so important.

Booking seats on the aisle on an airplane?

Getting up multiple times to urinate at night?

You know where every rest stop is between your home and long distance drives?

You are drinking alcohol and having to urinate after every glass?

Workouts interrupted by constant trips to the restroom?

You and your loved one are in a deep embrace and Oscar the Wonder Worm won't stand at attention. What the Fork?

At age 40, my primary doctor advised that we'd be watching PSA results as closely as my cholesterol.

The added bonus was every year he would strap on the surgical gloves and treat me to a digital rectal exam (DRE). This quick and easy, so he said, exam feels the prostate through the rectal wall for size, and roughness.

Men dread this exam as much as eating liver as a child.

Drop your drawers, bend over and relax (are you kidding me?). It's incredible that a trained urologist can detect anything but my discomforting grunts.

Apparently, pain is another indicator. I had over 29 years of nothing to worry about, until my PSA goes up, and yes, the DRE was painful.

My urologist was matter of fact about it. Book a biopsy and by the way you'll have to wait a month. Seems like there's a waiting list for biopsies. A month to think about an invasive search for prostate cancer was a lifetime. You'll learn more in chapter 10.

5
Prostate Stat. – Surviving Prostate Cancer

When addressing prostate cancer, it is important to consider the statistics from the National Institute of Health [6]:

* There were 164,690 new cases of Prostate Cancer in 2018, which represent 9.5% of all new cancer cases.

* One in nine men will be diagnosed with prostate cancer.

* Estimated deaths due to Prostate Cancer were 29,430 in 2018 representing 4.8% of all cancer deaths.

* 98.2% of men with a prostate cancer diagnosis survived five years (2008 -2014)

* 11.2% of men will be diagnosed with Prostate Cancer (one in nine men)

* Over 3,120,700 men in 2015 were living with Prostate Cancer.

The American Cancer Society's *Cancer Report* [7] in 2018 found that:

Prostate cancer death rates declined 52% from 1993 to 2015 among men.

Routine screening with the PSA blood test is no longer recommended because of concerns about high rates of over-diagnosis (finding cancers that would never need to be treated). Therefore, fewer cases of prostate cancer are now being detected.

This is not a victory dance, as I interpreted this report to say that PSA is not the only indicator of prostate cancer. The elevation of PSA leads to a biopsy and an MRI if cancer is detected. There's no resting with this cancer.

What is the cause of a cancer that all men face? A cancer that if not addressed will have catastrophic results before anything else can kill them.

When I started this journey I thought that there may be a simple answer like lifestyle, obesity, diet, or genetics (it is highly probable if your father or grandfather had prostate cancer then you and/or your brother will be diagnosed with it.)

That still doesn't explain how or why this cancer emerges in the prostate.

According to the American Cancer Society, "Researchers do not know exactly what causes prostate cancer. But they have found some risk factors like obesity, smoking, and genetics. They are trying to learn just how these factors cause prostate cells to become cancer."[8]

On a basic level, prostate cancer is caused by changes in the DNA of a normal prostate cell. DNA is the chemical in our cells that makes up our genes. Our genes control how our cells function. We usually look like our parents, because they are the source of our DNA, but DNA affects more than just how we look.

Some genes control when our cells grow, divide into new cells, and die:

Certain genes that help cells grow, divide, and stay alive are called oncogenes.

Genes that normally keep cell growth under control, repair mistakes in DNA, or cause cells to die at the right time, are called tumor suppressor genes.

Cancer can be caused in part by DNA changes (mutations) that turn on oncogenes or turn off tumor suppressor genes.

DNA changes can either be inherited from a parent or can be acquired during a person's lifetime."

On another note, Afro-Americans have a higher rate of prostate cancer.[9] This comes as a shocker to the medical community because everything had been based upon a Caucasian male. What has been discovered is a DNA marker that's different between the races, so traditional treatment options weren't successful.

After all of this it is reassuring to know that I have it, but don't know how I got it and now I have to treat it. Research tells me that diet plays a big role in the emergence of prostate cancer: obese (I thought I had big bones), love eating (thinking of those starving children in China).

What I do know is that something causes cell growth to mutate or accelerate ergo prostate cancer. I believe that growth in cells that already exist in my prostate is a result of events that might have been controlled early if acknowledged sooner, like frequent or painful urination, and erectile dysfunction.

As you will learn my MRI results revealed evidence of Benign Prostate Hyperplasia (enlarged prostate) in the past few years. It left me wondering if I had been more open about the issues I was having, could Prostate Cancer been delayed or not occurred at all?

Can diet be indicted for probable cause?

The jury is still out on this, but as I mentioned earlier in the book, the Asian culture has a low incidence of prostate cancer, attributable to a diet low in fat, high in fish and no red meat. So, eat like an Asian.

With a Western diet, it's just the opposite. When a high-fat and red meat-rich diet is introduced, the incidence of cancer goes up. This suggests that those "oxidative" foods cause mutations in the DNA, ergo prostate cancer.

Eating too many bad foods causes irreversible damage. Mom Tierno was a force of nature, a second generation Italian, a gourmet chef mother who taught us the joy of eating and cooking. She also got to be a sous chef with the late Julia Child.

She passed that talent on to her children including the love of pasta, meatballs, sausage, gnocchi(my favorite), a brisket to die for and a barbeque sauce for Pop's famous ribs; a carnivore's dream.

Now at 70, thanks to Karen, I'm devouring hummus with cauliflower, broccoli, carrots. Lots of fruits and vegetables rule the day, with chicken and lean red meat. Quinoa replaces rice. Breadsticks and French bread, are banned, except when we have guests. You get the picture. There's no going cold turkey, so iced tea replaces diet sodas. Wine and beer in moderation (OK, wine depending on the stressors of the day).

Finally, changing your diet has a positive effect on your heart health and blood pressure. Lose the weight, lower the fat impact to body mass, lower blood pressure and you lower the risk of heart attack.

The point is that men need to pay attention to what their body is telling them and not deny it as a passing event. They must also pay attention to what they put into their body.

This cancer is not tonsillitis or a virus that can be controlled or eliminated with a prescription or injection. It's a killer. The statistics don't lie. No amount of hope, prayers, and good wishes bely the truth. Here's a case-in-point with happier results. A resident here at Robson Ranch shared this experience having kept track of his PSA and communicating with his urologist:

"I just had my brush with prostate trouble last November. After my PSA level made a straight line graph from 2.7 to 5.1 over a period of three years, my urologist (Dr. John Jaderlund) recommended a biopsy procedure.

"As you know, getting your prostate shot full of holes is no fun. However, I barely managed to refrain from using my worst swear words in front of his female assistant. As it turned out, except for one borderline area, the results came back negative for cancer! Hallelujah! However, due to my enlarged prostate, the daily precautions you mentioned in the New Years blog are very familiar; the nearest restroom was always on my radar.

"The trip from the parking lot to the bathroom at Lowes felt like a red-light emergency. I'm lucky that some little old lady was not in the way. Now, with an alpha blocker prescription, life has improved two- or three-fold.

"I suspect that the borderline area on the margins will be watched closely as is the rise in PSA. Needless to say this was a great outcome for now."

6
The Andy Grove Intel Effect

Only the Paranoid Survive
-Andy Grove

Premise: no one talked about prostate cancer all that much until Andy Grove tackled his diagnosis with a vengeance.

Grove, the late former Intel CEO, blew the doors off the prostate cancer conversation by writing an article titled "Taking on Prostate Cancer" for *Fortune* in May, 1996. 10

Richard Tedlow in his book *Andy Grove, Life and Times of an American* 11 dedicated an entire chapter to Grove's prostate cancer: "Life is What Happens While You're Making Other Plans." Coincidentally, I was a an employee at Intel Corporation.

I bring this up because Will Fellner, a fellow ex Intel Golf Bum living in Florida reminded me about Andy's diagnosis and the magazine article.

Another example of support from my "army" of supporters. Keep in mind that this was 32 years ago and while the solutions (except robotic surgery) were still archaic like radical prostate surgery, cryosurgery was not available.

Radiation was the primary weapon in the prostate cancer battle. High-dose radiation was available in few locations like Seattle and New York. Brachytherapy (radioactive seeds) was also available. Andy didn't go into this battle alone or only half committed to his survival. An important lesson for all of us.

Andy Grove was one of the founders of Intel Corporation (a small microprocessor company in the Silicon Valley).

In 1994, his primary doctor retired and his new doctor ordered a battery of tests including PSA which he'd never discussed previously with his doctor. He had prostate cancer, and like any engineer he studied every aspect of the disease and available treatments.

In that groundbreaking 1996 article in *Fortune*, Andy pointed out the inconsistencies in prostate cancer treatments at the time. By the way, Michael Milken was a well known white-collar ex-convict who also was diagnosed with prostate cancer, and was responsible for developing strategies for finding the necessary funding to fight this "mens only" cancer.

Grove also believed strongly that diet may impact the DNA cell mutations which cause prostate cancer. While not proven, it's the anecdotal data that makes me believe in this approach. Asians have literally no cases of prostate cancer due to their diet. Low sugars, fat, and carbohydrates are the key.

When I was discharged from the hospital Dr. Bevan-Thomas was strong in his recommendation that I reduce or eliminate fats in my diet.

The establishment and acceptance of the fact that the PSA is the marker for diagnosing prostate cancer is a milestone in the history of the disease.

Reviewing all of the treatment options is a daunting challenge because frankly I didn't feel any worse for wear but clearly anxious because of the "alien cancer" growing within my prostate.

Andy's approach was a great role model to follow. There isn't a magic decoder ring. For the most part there is reliable data on every treatment option. I'm not on my deathbed nor am I even close, because of early detection. Thank you!

The one piece of advice Dr. Jaderlund and Dr. Bevan-Thomas gave me is there is no rush don't panic, but the clock is ticking on this time bomb. To highlight this, I was told that if I delayed until the first quarter of 2019 without hormone therapy, my PSA would likely double and a PSA of 10.0 means certainly bad news.

To paraphrase Andy, there are treatment solutions for your particular brand of prostate cancer. The outcomes vary based on physical condition and lifestyle.

The mortality rate varies as well. One thing for certain is that in every case the side effects suck. So one of the choices I had was to what degree-of-suck was I willing to live or tolerate?

Remember, the goals are to eliminate or stall the cancer, which will result in maintaining a quality of life minimizing incontinence if any, and restore sexual function (ED).

That's the priority I endorsed, assuming that solving ED was the lowest priority for the near term and made the most sense at age 69.

Of course, if a treatment option meant not being able to have an erection for four to five years, that option would be thrown in the round bin.

For example, cryotherapy was my first choice, but when told that the possibility of an erection would be best case in five years, it was immediately discounted.

Why do I bring up Andy Grove?

I met him in August of 1982 at an Intel Culture Orientation for new employees. I will always remember a new employee asking why Intel doesn't implement flex time. Andy responded that Intel had a great number of new college graduates (NCGs) who weren't disciplined enough to manage their time.

"We do have flex time," Andy exclaimed. "You start work anytime before 8:00 a.m. and you leave anytime after 5:00 p.m." The room was silent. I was fortunate to have the opportunity to work in a number of positions at Intel prior to retiring in 1999.

In June of 2007 at the Ex-Intel Golf Bum's annual golf tourney in Lake Tahoe. Carl Everett hosted the group at his home on North Lake Tahoe. We were honored with Andy's visit, along with the late Paul Otellini, and a host of legends from Intel's past.

Andy had beaten prostate cancer (or at least held it at bay), but in 2000 he was diagnosed with Parkinson's Disease. He attacked it as he had with prostate cancer, joining Michael J. Fox in challenging the medical community for a cure.

Andy made a point to shake hands with each of us and ask what we were doing with ourselves since leaving Intel. After thanking Andy for the opportunity to work at Intel, I shared my experience of owning a bed and breakfast and chairing a golf tourney for my parish.

Andy always listened intently and there was no bull shitting him. What he said to me was that he was impressed with everybody's new adventures and missions in life. I will always remember that encounter. The rest of the evening was a well-aged red wine blur.

7
The Love/Hate Relationship with your Urologist

I don't trust doctors. They are like golfers. Everyone has a different answer to your problem.
- Seve Ballesteros, *Seve: The Young Champion*

I've seen plenty of primary doctors and dentists over the years, but only one urologist. Until recently, my primary was male so doing a digital rectal exam became our annual "date," and we'd depart with "same time next year." We however were not friends in the personal sort of way.

It was a relationship based on my trust in his medical judgement and me hammering him with with questions, particularly when the Internet (the dumpster of all medical untruths) was available through YouTube and Google.

My PSA was always hovered around 2.0 and prostate cancer never crossed my mind. It wasn't until age 68 my PSA was slightly elevated 2.97 and my urologist said "let's keep an eye on this," insisting that it wasn't an aberration. He had over 35 years of experience, so I didn't protest.

The DRE wasn't pleasant. It didn't reveal any enlargement or roughness around the edges How he can tell this with a rubber glove on and feeling through my rectal wall is undoubtedly one of the wonders of modern medicine. Sort of a "trust me moment".

A year later, a routine blood test revealed a really elevated PSA of 5.9/4.0 with 4.0 + being of major concern. Of course I must have some Egyptian DNA as I immediately launched my ship "down denial."

I protested that it was something I ate, drank, or hanky panky with my wife. His response was blunt, brutal really: schedule the biopsy and let's deal with this "potential" situation.

I stalled and, he said "if you'd like to die a very unpleasant death, go ahead and stall; however, if it is prostate cancer it may be contained so let's move on it now."

Perhaps it was because he is a Texas Aggie or perhaps he's seen the worst of this disease and his arms-length blunt relationship was important to my understanding my predicament.

Doctors aren't your friends or buddies. Ronald Reagan once said "Trust but Verify." Trust your urologist, but do your research and ask questions no matter how trivial they sound to insure that he/she gives you the broadest number of options.

This isn't about taking the path of least resistance. Hold their feet to the proverbial fire and if uncomfortable get a second opinion or a third. You aren't negotiating for world peace or buying a house, or cattle. You are negotiating for the next 10-15-20 years of your life.

In the end, my urologist isn't a personal friend. I respect his professional behavior and blunt clear messages. They are in my best interest but I own the final decision regarding treatment.

Unlike our parents, who were raised to believe medical professionals were like Gods, we've learned to research and ask questions until we understand the situation.

Early detection allows you to research each treatment option with the surgeons and oncologists. Do not count on your urologist solely because he's the lighthouse warning you of the oncoming rocks if you don't steer clear into open calm seas.

8
Misery Loves Company... Give me a break!

Dealing with life's ups and downs is manageable, but life's sideways. Not so much.
- Mark A, Kwasny *Misery Loves Company*

Over the years it tickled me that my male friends' conversations slowly devolved into conversation about our health, which reminded me of my late mother's bridge group! Sore joints, knee or hip replacements, high or low blood pressure, Cholesterol (LDL/HDL), sleep apnea, and maybe frequent urination at night.

I don't remember any of my Ex-Intel Golf Bum buddies saying "Hey, good/bad news, my PSA results were good or bad. However if they had skin cancer, lasik, cataract surgery, or a heart bypass it was major news.

So why is it that the walnut-shaped capsule sitting just under our bladder, topped off by a seminal vessel and nerve bundles on each side, is never the topic of conversation (unless of course one is diagnosed with prostate cancer)? It tends to grow as men age.

It's hard to believe that the prostate can grow to the size of a lemon, but it is possible. We are barraged with commercials about homeopathic solutions to prostate health and even promises to increase your testosterone. Of course, we get to watch television commercials about Flomax or its generic but no mention of PSA.

A man's prostate health also can impact urination, erections and sexual prowess.

Ah, yes sexual prowess. If given a choice of life or sexual performance, it does give a man pause to reflect.

Of course, not being able to get and hold a "woody" is easily resolved by a prescription for Viagra, Cialis, or its compound pharmacy generic. I have yet to hear guy say prior to prostate surgery he was using either solution (More on this subject post-surgery).

It's personal and confidential as it should be. However after learning of so many of my friends, neighbors and associates battle with prostate cancer perhaps we should talk more about our "problem" in hopes that our shared experience will motivate more men to pay attention to their prostate health.

I had an experience recently where a friend asked me about my symptoms. One of them was frequent urination. I sloughed it off to drinking too much alcohol or liquids. He responded that he has frequent urination at night too but he thought it was due to his blood pressure medication.

I take blood pressure medication and one of its effects is NOT frequent urination. I asked if the doctor told him this and he said "no," once again proving my point that we don't deal with an issue head-on. Dream on, dream on.

Fortunately he has a physical soon and we reviewed a list of questions to address as it might be BPH (enlarged prostate) or worse. I saw in my MRI that I had BPH at some point and had I been more open with my primary doctor or urologist perhaps cancer might have been averted. Who knew? Now you do!

Remember the life you save might be the life of your best friend or your own.

9
Locating Your Libido (It's Not Where You Think)

Men are Pigs!
  -Wife of a friend (name withheld to protect the innocent)

Here's the genesis of that statement. I was being interviewed for the Cleveland, Ohio district manager's job for Intel.

Let's just say I was competing against myself because absolutely nobody wanted to move to the rust bucket city where the river caught fire back in the '70s.

After dinner I was whisked off to the Flats on the river where boats are docked side by side and yes there are boat bunnies too.

Our objective was to do market research about the culture of this blue collar mecca. Where do steel workers at the barely alive mills go for recreation and team building? Why of course, a cabaret, okay a men's club, okay a strip club. Don't be so judgemental.

The "floss" may be the latest dance craze today, but I never considered the possibility of a dancer flossing with a $65 tie back in 1984. I'll leave it up to your imagination.

Not only were men pigs, we were also accused of thinking with our cojones.

Fast forward to May of 2018. I had never given it much thought but my urologist briefed us on hormone therapy to reduce testosterone -- ie chemical castration. He then explained that contrary to popular male opinion libido originates in in your brain, not your crotch.

This explains why sexual predators who have chemical or physical castration don't stop being predators. Gives one pause doesn't it?

Eureka! There's a sex life after treatment! Maybe. Not to worry, your sex life may not be over. What a sigh of relief.

I'm not real sure if that was the best news for Karen my beautiful, voluptuous wife! The news certainly was a shock to her sensibilities as secretly she and her unnamed friend shared the same "men are pigs" view. but she was very happy with the good news is that I'd only be missing a body part but I'd still be a functioning male.

Karen kept saying it's all about ego to a guy and she's right. Prostate cancer is a big hit to a man's ego, there is no doubt about it.

This is a very positive message to a man to know that his sex drive/life may not be over because of prostate cancer. Each and every man out there should understand and know that this is an excellent opportunity for long kisses and warm embraces.

Section III

The Detour

10
Diagnosis

Denial is the unconscious belief that a certain fact is too terrible to face and therefore cannot be true. It turns challenges into crises, dilemmas into catastrophes.
- Richard S. Tedlow, *Denial, Why Business Leaders Fail to Look Facts in the Face-And What to Do About it*

Tedlow is correct about business leaders and denial but even men on a personal level face it when told they have prostate cancer.

If you're keeping score at home or in the cheap seats, here is my prostate timeline from 2016-2018:

Q4 2016
Lab tests indicate a slight increase in PSA from 2.0 to 2.97.

January 2017
Urologists orders another blood test PSA (watch closely) Lab Work results (PSA:2.25)

February 2018
Follow Up results (PSA: 5.94)Yikes! Awoooga, Awooga! The klaxon sounds off.

April 2018
Urologist visit (Blood work and DRE) Results (PSA: 5.08)

May 15, 2018
Biopsy

May 22, 2018
The verdict: "You have Cancer."

Having done some research, my reaction as a problem solver was to negotiate for "Watchful Waiting," in other words: stall. Dr. Jaderlund reviewed my results with authority.

One of my twelve cores was definitely cancerous with a Gleason score of 7 (4+3). The other eleven cores were marginal but probably cancerous. Having done the research I thought to myself, "that doesn't sound so bad," So, I asked about watchful waiting.

There was a very short pause and Dr. Jaderlund responded with resounding bluntness "You have Cancer. Bring your wife in for a review of options on the 29th."

FUBAR resounded in my head.

May 29, 2018
Review treatment options given my results

June 19, 2018
USMD Prostate Cancer Center meeting with Dr. Bevan-Thomas , surgeon, to discuss cryosurgery and Da Vinci robotic surgery)

July 16, 2018
MRI results

August 30, 2018
Radical Da Vinci robotic surgery to remove my prostate.

September 5, 2018
Clamping the catheter and testing my plumbing

September 6, 2018
Removal of the suprapubic catheter (external)

September 14, 2018
Meeting with surgeon to review surgery results.

December 11, 2018
First PSA test results since surgery <0.01 Undetectable

March 4, 2019
Second (six month) PSA test results <0.01 Undetectable.

I hope this demonstrates the importance of tracking your PSA numbers. Look at how my numbers jumped between January and April. Even the small rise in 2016 concerned by my urologist. Denial could have been fatal, as would procrastination and hesitancy.

My human (and masculine) instinct is avoidance: "I'll get to that later," like the PSA represents some weeds I have noticed creeping into my lawn, or a loose shingle on the roof.

Worse yet, my final instructions should I reach the end of my runway sooner than the numbers predict.

Ignore your PSA at your own peril.

And, oh. by the way man up and get an annual digital rectal exam (DRE). As uncomfortable as it sounds it's worse if you take a pass. The urologist looks for roughness and size of your prostate. If it is painful that's a clue. Don't disregard your PSA and DRE. Sounds like a broken record, doesn't it?

I've played golf with several men here at Robson Ranch who have had to deal with Prostate Cancer. Their starting point was double-digit PSA of over 20, the other was 16. When I asked them how that happened? Every time I was told they'd blown off the lab work and definitely didn't "like" the DRE. I kid you not.

11
Face your Fear, Face Your Foley Catheter

It really doesn't hurt, well it's a different kind of pain
- Tom Knox, neighbor and fellow prostate cancer survivor on the removal of his Foley catheter.

I took the low road trying to figure out what the worst case might be when looking at treatment options.

My biggest fear was having a Foley catheter and bag for any period of time. Every time I thought about it, a bolt of fear went through my groin. Ouch!

Research is something I really enjoy but no matter where I looked for treatment options other than radiation or hormone therapy, the dreaded Foley catheter was necessary.

For the uninformed, a tube is run up the penis and into the bladder. It's inflated on the bladder end and a bag is attached (small - to your leg ,and a large one primarily for sleeping).

The thought of having a straw shoved up my penis is painful in and of itself. There must be a procedure that doesn't involve a Foley catheter. USMD Cancer Center in Arlington, Texas developed a new suprapubic catheter directly below the belly button into the bladder. It looks like a well head in west Texas. Sold!

Karen, my loving wife and advocate was doing her best to understand my fear of the catheter but blurted out in front of my urologist, "for God's sake get over it. It's not an option. Consider it necessary for your survival you pussy."

Pussy? Well, that's not very lady like. Now that it she put it that way where's the straw pipe?

I faced my fear. When I awoke from surgery there was a Foley catheter installed and another connection for the external catheter. Fortunately the Foley catheter was only for 24 hours. No problem except that it would have to be removed after the external was connected to the bag.

Trust me when I say that a Foley catheter is uncomfortable and walking up and down the hospital halls wasn't my idea of fun.

Tom Knox drove down to Arlington to drive me home when I was discharged the next day. I couldn't leave until the Foley was removed so I had the entire day to think about that procedure.

When my surgeon finally showed up to discharge me I started sweating bullets in anticipation of the big "pull". He sent for "Gertha" the German nurse in to remove it. I don't know if she was German but she definitely commanded my attention as she pulled on the surgical gloves.

She chuckled as I asked her to be gentle. Tom had told me that it wouldn't hurt. It is a different kind of pain. She said "take a deep breath and exhale." The rest is relief after a muffled scream. Tom chuckled, no giggled….very funny!

Discharged with a bag strapped to my leg I head home with Tom at the helm/wheel. By the time we arrive back at the ranch the bag is full. What the hell! How does one generate so much urine in so little time?

I quickly switched to the supersize bag. Overnight, it was completely full, much to my surprise. Fast forward 5 days and it's time to clamp the catheter and test the plumbing. Of course no experience with a catheter bag would be complete without looking down and seeing what looks like a plasma bag!

Apparently I strained when I had a bowel movement and all kinds of stuff broke loose. Needless to say visions of Nurse Gertha with a 24 inch straw in her hand grinning from ear to ear were dancing in my head.

Fortunately, the visiting nurse calmed me down and called the surgeon's office. The RN calmed me down and said this was normal as "stuff" breaks loose and gets flushed out of the system. By the quantity of "stuff" I expected to see an organ splash down in the catheter bag. Several hours later the clarity returned to the flow into the bag. Whew!

On the 5th day I clamped the catheter and tested my plumbing.

Eureka! A steady stream! I almost passed out from relief. My neighbor Tom Knox took me back to USMD Cancer Center to have the suprapubic catheter removed.

What kind of "pain" would this entail when you pull 20" of tubing out of your bladder through an incision just below your belly button? The RN told me that I'll feel a small discharge of urine but no significant pain.

I imagined a creature from *Alien* emerging from the depths of my bladder. The RN ask me to take a deep breath and release it. The tube came out quickly with a geyser of urine, but no alien. It actually sounded like he tapped a keg. My kingdom for a beer.

It's been ten months since the operation and removal of the catheter. No drips, leaks, or flash floods. I don't use a pad or briefs for protection as of New Years Eve! Back to boxer shorts, swinging free at last!

I manned up to the catheter and won! Who's the pussy, now?

12
The Gleason Score Roulette Wheel

Alice, I'm going to send you to the moon
- Jackie Gleason, *The Honeymooners*

Those of us who are Baby Boomers remember the television show The Honeymooners. Whenever Jackie Gleason as Ralph Kramden got frustrated with his wife Alice he'd threaten to "send her to the moon" a veiled threat of course but humorous in Ralph's delivery. (Note: This is not politically correct today)

A Gleason score has nothing to do with Ralph Kramden but I can assure you that the anticipation of your Gleason score will send you to the moon and back.

The Gleason score is a quantitative way to analyze cancer cells viewed under a microscope to determine their severity.

Cells that are well differentiated are given a low grade (2,3,4). Poorly differentiated cells are given a high grade (8,9,10). Moderately differentiated cells fall into a middle group (5,6,7)

In the prostate cancer batting order, the Gleason score follows the PSA.

Step One: Your PSA is a four or above.

Step Two: the Digital Rectal Exam (DRE) is either of concern or not to the urologist but he must check for roughness and size of the prostate. When your primary doctor or urologist pulls on the surgical glove and lubricant and says "bend over here it comes again" (BOHICA). "Nothing unusual here, he says go ahead and schedule a biopsy." My PSA was 5.5 so it was on to:

Step Three: an invasive biopsy to determine your Gleason score. This procedure takes no more than 15 minutes. It is an outpatient procedure usually done without knocking you out but it does deaden the rectal wall.

What? No valium or anesthesia? 12-15 Minutes of rectal terror? Yes, he compared it to a dentist deadening the jaw but I failed to see the difference with a needle inserted into my anal orifice.

Oh, Did I mention that an ultrasound rod is inserted in said anal orifice first? This is to take the fun out of guessing where my prostate "walnut" is located on the other side of the rectal wall.

Simply stated the biopsy is a means to sample the prostate by obtaining cores of tissue by way of a needle with a spring action corer so that they can be examined in a lab for cancer.

The number of cores taken in my case was twelve. It actually covers four quadrants of the prostate to insure that the sampling is accurate.

Twelve? Really? 3 cores x 4 quadrants = 12. Seriously, it seems like a lot for a walnut shaped capsule.

A dozen pricks is never a pleasant experience and it only hurts when I think about it.

Let's just say the urologist has to go through your rectum and penetrate the rectal wall to reach the prostate. Get the picture? Click, click, click I can't get that sound out of my mind.

Dr. Jaderlund was a professional at doing a 12-15 minute biopsy. He narrated each step. Of course, he embellished a bit when he commented that the size of my prostate was normal or small.

Staying optimistic, I asked what the odds were that it's cancerous. His response was, "good, maybe 50-50." I'm doomed!

It's a toss up which hurts more, the actual biopsy or the anxiety waiting a week for my results as the roulette wheel spins. Will that ball land on high, low, or moderate grade results? Post biopsy, it only hurts when I think about it. Click,click,click.

My Gleason score was a 7 (4+3) with one core 15% cancer and 8 out of the 12 cores marginal. Ultimately my prostate was 15% cancerous and the remaining cores were on the edge.

A Gleason score of 7 is in the "moderate" range so it placed me in an intermediate risk group. T1C diagnosis means the cancer was contained in the capsule and in the left quadrant.

Early detection before cancer cells break out of the prostate is critical. It also offers the most options for treatment.

If it happened to be on the low risk side, perhaps I could negotiate "watchful waiting" or do nothing except a annual PSA test and of course another fun filled biopsy next year.

There would be no negotiation here as the Gleason score was a 7 (4+3) where the cancerous cells were larger (4) than the smaller (3) so here I was in the middle of the intermediate risk group. I just had to ask anyway.

When talking to prostate cancer patients and survivors it's important to not ignore the Gleason score in the conversation.

Recently, I spoke to a gentleman who had been diagnosed by the same urologist and was told that "watchful waiting" was recommended.

I felt a bit envious but when I asked about the Gleason score he told me that it was a 6 (3+3), or low risk.

"Good news" only delays the inevitable in my opinion.

It means there is no rush to take more definitive action. A biopsy every year if the PSA continues to go up isn't something I would would call a win.

Another associate of mine also chose watchful waiting and less than a year later he was undergoing radiation treatments. Once prostate cancer cells break through the prostate capsule and into the lymph nodes all bets are off.

Another neighbor of mine who is seventy four years old chose watchful waiting but didn't know his Gleason score? Hmmm.

Another neighbor chose radiation in his mid 70s. He's held the cancer at bay but the treatments took their toll on his overall health.

Keep in mind that age and health play an important role in making watchful waiting on treatment option decision.

We spent over a week night and day studying everything we could find out about treatment options.

The fun is just beginning because your urologist will only explain your options and has no dawg in this hunt. Be prepared to grill him mercilessly to understand the options in front of you because once you make a decision there is no turning back.

On a side note, I applied for an additional insurance policy recently and the underwriter was surprised that I knew that my diagnosis was T1C, Gleason score of 7 (3+4) and my recent PSA results were <0.01 undetectable.

The underwriter said 90% of the applications who stated they were diagnosed with prostate cancer didn't know their numbers. Wow! How can you not know your prostate cancer numbers?

Are you Egyptian? Are you in denial (in the Nile)? Unbelievable! Write them down for God's sake! My "history" of cancer resulted in a denial. So much for no one is denied life insurance.

What I have learned is that prostate cancer is very slow growing if diagnosed early. What is your PSA? What was it last year?

Opinions are free, but do what is in the best interest of getting all of your questions (not concerns) answered. If you are chasing your "correct" answer save yourself some time and heartache. Which treatment gives you the best chance of living life to the fullest and longest. How much "suck" are you willing to live with?

Dr. Jaderlund my urologist spent over *two and a half hours* reviewing my biopsy results, the data on mortality rates, and of course my treatment options. First and foremost he stressed the goals of prostate cancer treatment:

1) Eliminate, delay, or contain the cancer's growth

2) Maintain or improve quality of life (minimize incontinence), and,

3) Restore sexual functionality (erections, woodies, boners)

As prepared as we thought we were, I left this meeting with my head spinning, not willing to accept radical prostate surgery. Appointments were set with Dr. Bevan-Thomas a cryo surgeon and da Vinci robotic surgeon.

I originally had an appointment with a radiologist but canceled it after my meeting with Dr. Bevan-Thomas. Thank you, Karen, for taking great notes!

13
This is Your New Life

Today, you have the opportunity to transcend from a disempowered mindset to an empowered reality of purpose-driven living. Today is a new day that has been handed to you for shaping.
— Steve Maraboli

While I accepted my diagnosis, I was looking ahead to what my life would be like following surgery. I chose to take the high road, praying for the best outcome.

My neighbor Tom, a prostate cancer survivor of over two years since his da Vinci surgery, impressed upon me that this experience does not result in a new normal but a new lease on life (as in changed).

This was very perplexing, and I wrestled with that one pre-surgery. Good, bad, or really bad outcome(s); that was my mental challenge moving forward.

Post-surgery planning required attention to what-not-do versus what-you-can-do for the first eight weeks. No lifting of weights over 15-20 pounds.

Pay attention to urinary patterns. Take stool softeners and don't strain during bowel movements. Who wants to get a hernia while taking a dump?

No incontinence, no diapers or pads, a few incisions, well, no erections for a while is certainly a change but given the alternative and the availability of magic pills and other solutions hopefully this will be rectified soon. No kissing and telling but Karen and I love each other more each day of our life's journey.

My fraternity brother Ron Sorter, one helluva funny guy, a Vietnam Veteran with the coolest collection of prosthetic legs calls it threading the eye of the needle. It takes mental clarity, not brute force.

I don't wake up each day and pray for a better life. I thank God, the Virgin Mary, St. Joseph, St. Francis, St. Christopher , St. Michael and all of the saints for this great life. It's all about gratitude, not platitudes ("I wish, I want, I need"). While not completely laser-focused, my life has a new improved perspective and a new plan for finishing life strong.

Steve Farrar wrote the book *Finishing Strong*.[12] His cover says it all, "Finding the Power to go the distance". I urge every man to read this book should he experience temptation as well as depression in your life.

I originally bought this book following an epiphany in my life which involved a major "redeployment" at Intel Corporation in our field sales force, a recommitment to my marriage to Karen, and following my own advice to employees to get their personal house in order.

In December of 1995 we bought The Hanford House Bed and Breakfast Inn in Sutter Creek, CA. Thirteen years later, we sold it during the great recession.

When I retired the first time at age fifty in 1999, the goal was to manage the inn to profitability not knowing that there would be an energy crisis in California, a workmen's compensation insurance debacle statewide, the tragedy of 9/11 which resulted in more travelers driving versus flying and a fire. It seems like we experienced everything except locusts.

I tried my hand at business coaching. I tried my hand at business coaching from 2008 -2015 and developed a successful practice in Houston and later in Sacramento. The business was difficult to sustain with my parents' failing health and numerous trips to the east coast.

Fast forward to 2015. I had been hired to manage three 1-800-Got-Junk? Franchises in Texas by a self proclaimed absentee owner/entrepreneur.

This accomplished our goal of seeking asylum in Texas, a state with better economics, ie. no personal income tax, lower home prices, lower gas prices, you get the picture.

It also enabled Karen to visit her mother and siblings in Oklahoma City and Tulsa. We had been moving like gypsy travelers for over 40 years.

My late parents had lived on the east coast while we were galavanting around the country. Their passing taught me that we needed to get closer to family rather than farther away since we had no children.

The job sucked on so many levels and tested my ethical boundaries with an owner who had no people skills, who cared more about establishing policies and procedures.

Yet, he was in love with the 70% gross margins padding his bank account. "Once we have policy and procedures in place, we'll worry about the culture of this company." (paraphrased) Comprendo?"

Parting company in March, 2017 was a huge relief

During this period the stress was taking its toll and I maintain that the owner's behavior had impact on my health when my PSA as it began to creep up in 2017.

A year later in January, 2018, my PSA rose to 5.9 which slapped me upside the head. A second PSA test 30 days later was unchanged, so it was into the urologist and the rest is history.

If I were to look to anything that may have caused my elevated PSA it would be the stress of that management job. Not a hunch....just fact.

14
Your Treatment Scenarios: They All Suck

*What has been will be again,
what has been done will be done again;
there is nothing new under the sun.*
Ecclesiastes 1:9

Once you have a cancer diagnosis, the treatment options will rush at you like a Texas flash flood. Your head will spin.

Every day you will hear about something new, or a well-meaning family member will send you a link to a cure, a silver bullet or a miracle from Heaven.

I can't tell you what to do except don't do nothing.

Don't suffer "paralysis by analysis" and let the decision making derail you from moving forward to something.

I am sharing my story in this book as a way to show you that there is a way forward. Prostate cancer will throw everything it has at you. Are you ready?

What follows are all the prostate cancer treatment options I considered, given my diagnosis. They are not recommendations. Your medical history and your cancer diagnosis are most likely different from mine. "Your mileage may vary," as they say in the car commercials.

Remember what the goals are. They should guide you as you stand at the plate swatting at the white ball of cancer hurling at you at breakneck speed.

1) Eliminate, delay, or contain the cancer's growth;

2) Maintain or improve quality of life (minimize incontinence), and

3) Restore sexual functionality (erections, woodies, boners)

My role as an advocate is to help you wait for the ideal pitch, and stop wasting your swings. To continue with a baseball analogy, there is no grand slam "home run" treatment option out there (yet). At best, you lay down a bunt and beat out the throw at first base. You steal second, and third, and then suddenly the third base coach is waving you in to home plate.

And sometimes your run is not enough to win the game. It may result in a tie or extra innings. But one thing you are not doing is sitting in the dugout, wishing you were out on the field, under the lights.

I recommend Dr. Patrick Walsh's *Guide to Surviving Prostate Cancer*. Dr. Walsh presents clearly understandable "short stories" in each chapter, then follows with facts, figures, and descriptions of all of the known options to date.

It's the book I relied upon for four straight months. I continue to rely on it today as an excellent resource book. I've summarized these stages from my research and will discuss treatment options that I considered in my case. The American Cancer Society also has an excellent online summary of the prostate cancer stages with treatment considerations. 13

There are four stages of prostate cancer : the PSA, Gleason Score, and the stage (T 1-4), spreading to lymph nodes (N+), and to bone (M+) For example mine was a T1C, N=0, T=0

T1: This stage is not outside the prostate capsule. Usually found after a PSA >4.0 and a needle biopsy ergo T1C. Treatment options range from watchful waiting , radiation, or radical prostatectomy.

T2(a,b,c): This stage indicates cancer anywhere from less than half to both lobes of the prostate. Options range from active surveillance, radical prostatectomy, or radiation therapy. Age plays a big part in treatment. Hormone therapy is used in all cases.

T3, T4: The cancer has penetrated the prostate capsule wall and involves the seminal vesicles. In Stage 3, the cancer hasn't spread to the bladder or rectum so all options are on the table. Age is critical because of other possible medical issues. In those cases men often choose active surveillance or hormone therapy by itself.

T4 Cancer has already spread to nearby areas like the bladder or rectum, lymph nodes, or even bones. Bottom line T4 cancer is incurable but is treatable with a focus on quality of life. All options are on the table including treatment for bone cancer with the latest chemotherapy, external radiation focused on bones, or radiopharmaceutical like strontium 89, samarium 153, or radium 223.

15
Elevated PSA but no Cancer

My story may not be your story. Here is a scenario worth talking about. This may be the gateway to watchful waiting or very good timing when PSA is elevated, a biopsy is called for and no cancer is detected. There are several approaches.

I met someone who had a follow up 3D MRI (yes with an ultrasound rod placed you guessed it) and cancer was discovered on the backside of the prostate. This survivor opted for robotic surgery to be described later.

The second case had all of the symptoms described earlier. A biopsy was conducted which had negative results (no cancer). His urologist recommended that he be treated for the symptom with an alpha blocker for BPH.

According to the Mayo Clinic, alpha blockers relax the muscle in the prostate and bladder neck There are five medications such as terazosin (Hytrin), doxazosin (Cardura), tamsulosin (Flomax), alfuzosin (Uroxatral), and silodosin (Rapaflo). 14

In 2017, I was prescribed Flomax. It helped reduce trips to the bathroom at night. There is controversy about Flomax regarding long term effects but obviously it didn't slow the elevation of my PSA. It has no impact on PSA according to my urologist.

16
Hormone Therapy

This chapter is an abridged discussion about Hormonal Therapy from Dr. Patrick Walsh's book *Guide to Surviving Prostate Cancer*. 15

Doctors use hormonal therapy in specific situations and it's discouraged in cases like mine where the cancer is localized in the prostate capsule:

* If the cancer is locally advanced it is used in concert with radiation treatments and only for a defined period of time.

* If there is a rising PSA level after primary treatments with surgery or radiation and finally,

* Men with metastatic disease

Hormone therapy is also referred to as Androgen Deprivation Therapy (ADT) which basically shuts down the hormones that feed the prostate nourishing the cancer.

Let's be clear hormone therapy for a man is chemical castration (as my voice goes up a dozen octaves). By driving the testosterone to zero it stalls the cancer's growth.

In some cases, an orchiectomy (surgical castration) is called for to guarantee the testosterone is reduced to castrate range or zero.

Like a weed killer, it starves the cancer cells. Life without giblets and feeling much better is a good outcome.

One of my cousins had no choice because the cancer had spread and the best doctors in the world suggested NOT to remove his prostate but rather radiation (45 treatments). In addition he had hormone therapy (Quarterly) and he's doing just fine. He's alive, playing golf with his buddies and enjoying trips with his family.

My message is to understand how hormone therapy is used in your fight and to only use it if necessary. Do not succumb to your urologist who may propose hormone therapy when in fact it is not necessary. If you are trying to delay your decision, it "might" be helpful in slowing the growth of cancer cells, but there are no guarantees.

You need to ask why, how, where, and when it is used in your case. Obviously, I was fortunate and it was not considered necessary. It was even discouraged by my surgeon at USMD Prostate Cancer Center given my circumstances.

Is there the possibility of cancer resistance to hormone therapy? Absolutely, when the cells have metastasized. Only recently have prescription therapies been tested to meet this challenge. I didn't spend much time researching this situation as I was fortunate to only be diagnosed T1C. Again every turn in this journey there is an outcome which begets another outcome so the battle rages on.

17
Do Nothing (and Die)

There is one truth if you choose to do nothing . You will be called out at the plate taking that third strike rather than swing at a high and fast "meatball". It will hurt, no it will be very painful because you let not only yourself down, but your family, friends, and supporters down as well.

Once the cancer moves out of the containment area or "capsule" of your prostate, it can head straight to your lymph nodes, the bloodstream, the spinal column and bone joints. You get the picture. Then you die.

It's that simple and that real. No breakthrough research or "revolutionary" mint tea or burning-sage-in- your-backyard ritual will ever change the rapid and brutal pathway the cancer will take upon exiting your prostate

If I told you a meteorite was going to strike your house next Tuesday, you would most likely find someplace else to be (most likely before the weekend and most likely in another town).

If you have a high PSA and a high Gleason score and other cancer symptoms, the last thing you want to do is put your feet up in your recliner, order pizza and wait for the end like it's a normal weeknight.

18
Homeopathic Medicine

According to Wikipedia, "Homeopathy or homœopathy is a system of alternative medicine created in 1796 by Samuel Hahnemann, based on his doctrine of like cures like, a claim that a substance that causes the symptoms of a disease in healthy people would cure similar symptoms in sick people." [16]

Homeopathic medicines are made from plant, chemical, mineral or animal sources. Coincidentally this the most prevalent in the treatment of cancer.

Wait for it…There is no scientific or medical evidence that it can cure cancer or work as a cancer treatment.

I've been told stories about men who chose homeopathic methods and over-the-counter prostate supplements. In fact several of my friends told me about this herb and that herb or the latest prostate-reducing solution with testosterone enhancing powers. Most, if not all are not FDA-approved . Did you know that there are over 80,000 supplements on the market?

Ginseng cannot possibly help you win the battle over cancer, despite the pseudo-academic claims. Watch out for supplements that claim to "inhibit prostate cancer progression, fight inflammation and free radicals, and reduce tumor development and volume."

Here's a baker's dozen of seductive supplements I found on the Web, all with reasonable "science" behind them:

AHCC (Basidiomycete mushrooms)
Cayenne (capsaicin)
Cruciferous vegetables (broccoli, kale, cauliflower)
DIM diindolylmethane
Curcumin (tumeric)
Ginseng
Green tea
Modified citrus pectin
Omega-3
Pomegranate
Resveratrol (red wine, red grapes)
Vitamin D (daily requirements only)

Save your money. Write your Will and final instructions. Buy a Neptune Society (Cremation) membership, or your cemetery plot. Don't forget to tell your urologist what you are doing. He or she need a good laugh.

Seriously, I have never put much stock in over the counter homeopathic solutions. The first reason is cost and marketing. They are too expensive, make unrealistic promises, and they are not FDA-approved.

Secondly, I have a problem with the mix of ingredients. If you have high blood pressure, you don't need a lightning jolt of caffeine or ginseng negating my my blood pressure medicine.

Also, these products are marketed to remedy low testosterone, even when your blood tests are normal or showing high "T." Yet another clue is that it is not a valid remedy.

There is no scientific or medical proof that any of these homeopathic remedies cure or treat cancer.

19
Functional Medicine

The Institute for Functional Medicine defines functional medicine as "a systems biology–based approach that focuses on identifying and addressing the root cause of disease. Each symptom or differential diagnosis may be one of many contributing to an individual's illness." [17]

Those trained in functional medicine typically study the physiology by utilizing testing to track conditions over time. For example, digestion, food allergies/intolerances, and even hormone balance.

So what's the difference between functional medicine, naturopathic medicine, and traditional medicine?

First and foremost, unctional and naturopathic edicine are used in an integrative way to focus on wellness and prevention rather than traditional medicine using pathology versus a systematic approach.

This is arguable and frankly having been diagnosed with prostate cancer, I was interested in rooting it out rather than it's root cause. So the remainder of the therapies are from traditional medicine. However, if you don't have prostate cancer I think considering these alternatives have merit.

20
Naturopathic Medicine

I had never heard of naturopathic medicine and it was an eye-opener.

It piqued my curiosity because a close friend's wife graduated from a noted Naturopathic School in Southern California.I read Dr. Mary Mielke's blogs and studied Naturopathic medicine potential.

I interviewed Dr Mielke, ND (Naturopathic Doctor) and Dr. Tiffany Bloomingdale, ND at their offices at the Richmond Natural Medicine clinic in Richmond, VA to better understand the role they play when working with cancer patients.

According to Dr. Mielke, "our practice provides naturopathic supportive care for patients at all stages of their cancer diagnosis and treatment. This includes therapies which enhance the effectiveness of conventional treatment, reduce the side effects of their therapies and improves their overall quality of life.

"Patients do best when receiving a combination of conventional and naturopathic care. We provide counseling and integrated care plans for patients who may be any place along the continuum – cancer prevention, pre-biopsy, post-diagnosis, early treatment, post-treatment, and maintenance.

"We use basic lab tests to monitor what we call the 'terrain' of the individual. We all develop cancerous cells, but not everyone develops a tumor. In naturopathic medicine, we support the health of the whole person such that their 'terrain' is not amenable to cancer proliferation, helping the immune system remain effective at eliminating dysplastic cells."

One of the tests used by naturopathic doctors is the DUTCH Test (Dried Urine Test for Comprehensive Hormones.) This test is not used to diagnose or cure any specific disease, per se.

The DUTCH Test focuses on which hormones are out of range including those that are age dependent. The DUTCH test is also the most detailed way to assess your adrenal function and sex hormones.

The adrenal part of the test measures your free cortisol at four different times during the day, as well as cortisone and total cortisol production according to Precision Analytical, Inc.

Digging deeper, Dr. Mielke pointed me to the Oncology Association of Naturopathic Physicians (OncANP) - a distinct healthcare profession focused on whole health solutions for cancer patients.

Their approach is non-invasive and may include acupuncture, botanical medicine, clinical nutrition, physical medicine and lifestyle counseling.

This is a collaborative integrated approach which is combined with the traditional treatments by the oncologist and is referred to as integrative oncology.

OncANP's surveys estimate that over 80% of people with cancer are choosing this combination of natural and supportive therapies in conjunction with conventional treatments.

There are naturopathic doctors in almost every state, but not all specialize in oncology supportive care. And, of course, many health insurance plans do not cover naturopathic medicine at this time. The DUTCH tests range in price from $299 to $499.

21
Watchful Waiting (WW)

Watchful waiting is not a religious group that comes to your door handing out devotional tracts. In the last few years, Watchful waiting has become a popular course of action, or inaction, if you prefer. In my opinion it is one way to put off the inevitable but if you are under age 70, look at all of your options.

Your urologist will explain that if your biopsy reveals prostate cancer and the Gleason Score is 3+3, that puts you in a low risk group (versus mine 4+3 =7).

Depending on your age and health watchful waiting may be recommended.

If you are not healthy enough to undergo other treatment options this may be a course of action. PSA tests will still be required and if your PSA is elevated beyond the initial diagnosis, a biopsy and MRI would probably be the next steps.

I know several men who are doing watchful waiting. One didn't have to wait very long. His scores went up over a one year period and he chose radiation, so keeping a pulse on the situation is important. Again your age and physical condition may be the deciding factors in accelerating treatment options that make sense for you based on your "life's runway".

Watchful waiting has had an impact on the drop in deaths due to prostate cancer. It has also slowed the rate of radical surgeries over time.

Just keep in mind that your age and physical condition are important considerations. Hormone therapy may be recommended but if you are in good health don't do it because of the risks of developing heart disease, diabetes, cognitive impairment. Recent studies indicate that there's no benefit to hormone therapy versus the risks.

In summary, watchful waiting is "wait and see". You only get treated if you need it.

22
Active Surveillance (AS)

If you don't mind knowing that you have prostate cancer, active surveillance may be considered with the following caveats:

* Follow up biopsies every year to fifteen months.

* Digital Rectal Exams

* PSA tests every three to six months.

Walsh's book discusses combining AS with drugs but be sure to fully understand the implications and consequences.

Dietary and lifestyle changes have a better chance of stabilizing your situation. Just remember, if the situation warrants then treatment is not to be delayed.

Anecdotally, I know of the case of a California male in his early 60's, who was diagnosed Gleason 3+3 T1c and opted for active surveillance. His PSA has been consistently, but slowly, rising. This individual is a trained medical professional (podiatric physician) and a public health instructor at a local university. He has let us know that this book has been especially informative as he considers his options.

23
Prostate Popsicles (Cryotherapy - Cryoablation)

Think prostate popsicle
USMD Prostate Cancer Center in Arlington, Texas.

That's the best explanation of cryosurgery I've seen so far. Those same folks have an excellent cryosurgery video that will either make you scream or pass out.

Set up the quote below:

"Cryosurgery is a breakthrough prostate cancer treatment that is a proven, minimally invasive alternative to surgical treatments and radiation treatment.

"Cryosurgery incorporates the use of slim probes known as 'cryoprobes' that periodically deliver cycles of extremely cold and warm temperatures to repeatedly freeze and thaw cancerous cells within and surrounding the prostate gland– ultimately destroying the cancerous cells.

"Utilizing ultrasound technology to guide the treatment, the probes are strategically inserted through the skin and placed in and around the prostate.

"This tactical placement of the cryoprobes allows your surgeon to target the prostate gland while minimizing damage to surrounding tissue.

"Through completion of two or more freeze/thaw cycles, cancerous cells are killed and the remaining tissue is either absorbed by the body or remains as scar tissue, no longer posing a threat to the patient.

"The cryosurgery procedure is performed under general or epidural anesthesia. Because this procedure is relatively short (usually lasting 1 to 1.5 hours) and is minimally invasive in nature, you will experience reduced side-effects, including incontinence and/or impotence, and a faster recovery. Many patients are discharged the same day as their procedure or the following day.

"Following cryosurgery, patients are instructed to administer ice packs to the scrotal and perineal areas for three to five days and will be instructed to take prescription or over-the-counter anti-inflammatory medications for up to one week. Patients will be equipped with a suprapubic or foley catheter for up to one week following the procedure." [18]

Unfortunately, even after collecting data for thirty years, urologists are undecided about this approach. The argument is that there is not enough long term data comparing this to other treatments and mortality rate predictors.

The USMD Prostate Cancer Center in Arlington, Texas has Cryotherapy as an option and presents a good case for it. My conclusion is that cancer treatment centers focus on core specialties and this may not be one of them.

For example, The National Comprehensive Cancer Network doesn't recommend this option for routine localized prostate cancer.

That was an eye opener for me and there are secondary considerations. The first is not having the ability to have an erection for up to five years (ouch). Plus, going home feeling like I got kicked square in my cojones as Dr. Bevan-Thomas explained it.

The thought of long sharp probes being inserted through my perineum didn't thrill me either. In addition that a suprapubic catheter (external) would be required for up to a week. When it comes to catheters there's no escaping this torture.I know, I know "Man Up " and quit being a pussy!".

Of course, if I chose cryosurgery and the prostate cancer came back, the surgeon said he could perform a salvage operation. What am I? A sunken treasure ship? Well mates, even your innards are salvageable.

24
Radiation and Brachytherapy: Keep Your Powder Dry

Radiation has been around since 1904, when it was introduced in the U.S. after being pioneered in Europe. Radiation involves placing radium applicators around the prostate. Effective at shrinking tumors, it was a short-term and mostly palliative (relieving pain) treatment. [19]

This was true even after X-Rays beams were used, followed by "seeds" implanted into the prostate directly. In the 1940s, hormone therapy emerged as did high power beams which increased the intensity of the radiation treatment and focused on the tumor(s).

This resulted in external beam therapy and inserting radioactive seeds directly into the prostate (brachytherapy). Both were found to be effective in destroying the cancer cells. The seeds approach on the west coast has been widely used while here in North Texas not so much.

The 1990s saw great strides with three specific therapies:

* Three--dimensional conformal radiation therapy (3-DCRT)

* Intensity-modulated radiation therapy (IMRT), and most recently

* Image-guided radiation therapy (IGRT)

So why not radiation therapy in my case?

The first was my age, 69 years old. Most importantly, the cancer was contained in the prostate capsule. Radical prostate surgery should remove all or most of the cancer but it's not guaranteed.

There are also practical considerations. In my case it would require a 10-15 minute burst five days a week for eight weeks. It would also require a 100-mile round-trip daily. I was told some patients rent a mobile home and park at the hospital, returning home on the weekends.

I chose to keep radiation in reserve if needed in the future. As the frontiersmen used to say, "keep your powder dry." Wait until you actually need it.

One more observation about brachytherapy. It is used in conjunction with external beam treatments. Not only do you have seeds implanted into your prostate, you will require up to 18 treatments. One of my closest friends chose that method and it's worked out for him.

Hold on to your helmet, Buck Rogers. There are a number of interesting and hopefully powerful treatments I read about like CyberKnife, proton therapy, and high-tntensity focused ultrasound (HIFU).

Depending on your particular diagnosis add them to your list of questions for your urologist and/or cancer treatment centers.

In his *Guide to Surviving Prostate Cancer,* Dr. Patrick Walsh has the most current discussions on all new treatments through 2018.

A one-day high intensity treatment is offered in New York and/or Seattle so travel and time commitment are required.

25
What Me, MRI? Magnetic Resonance Imaging

Some people say that when you get knocked down, you should get up again. I say you should stay down and admire the ceiling.
- Mark Kwasny, *Misery Loves Company*

Author Note: This is my story and a very detailed description of my Da Vinci robotic surgery can be found in Chapter 26. These are the steps leading up to it.

Are you FUBAR (totally screwed) when diagnosed with this Men's Only Club disease?

The answer is (pun intended), it depends.

Previously, I discussed the importance of your PSA score, DRE, and if necessary a biopsy. This is not a fun experience. Prostate cancer presents a myriad of options and side effects (which quite frankly suck).

I am not a medical doctor or surgeon. I am a prostate cancer survivor, so it's important that you understand the goals of prostate cancer treatment based upon what stage of cancer you find yourself.

Fortunately, I was diagnosed with Stage T2C, which meant the cancer wasn't obvious through a DRE, but because of elevated PSA it was discovered by a biopsy.

The recommended treatments for my case included radiation, cryotherapy, or radical prostatectomy.
No hormone therapy was called for, and before making a decision, an MRI was a required next step.

The diagnosis for me was not a gut punch or huge surprise.

Over the course of the past 18 months, I saw my PSA go up. When it syrpassed the score of 4.0, I was communicating with my urologist online. It took two months to get an appointment for the PSA follow up tests.

Then, there was another month to schedule the biopsy, and that time was well spent playing Pickleball, praying and researching the options I might have when I receive the final diagnosis.

Make no mistake about this life challenge. It is a fight but no one with cancer fights alone. If you try to fight it alone you can expect a long a painful death.

This was a detour on my Route 66 road trip to my seventh decade with 70 in my sights. I am visualizing the U.S. Open at Pebble Beach, and the annual Lake Tahoe Ex-Intel Golf Bums tourney in June, 2019..

But first it's threading the eye of the needle.

Why an MRI?- Who or What do you choose?

Magnetic resonance imaging (MRI) is a diagnostic tool that uses magnetic fields and radio waves to produce a detailed image of the prostate. It also means forty five frightening minutes in a tube which I never could understand.

If they are looking at my prostate why does my head have to be in the tube? Yes, I'm claustrophobic and while not painful an MRI is very close to the invasive biopsy

After the MRI was completed, Karen and I headed to lunch, pending a review of the results with my surgeon at 2:30 p.m..

Ushered into the private room by a nurse, Dr. Bevan-Thomas put the images up on a screen and identified the cancerous portion of my prostate. He also identified scarring due in part to benign prostate hyperplasia (BPH), or enlarged prostate.

We went into this meeting armed to the teeth with our research and set on cryosurgery. We reviewed all of the "what ifs" and important things like recovery time, and when can I go back to Pickleball and golf?

What does it feel like the first three to five days? (response "it's like you got kicked in the nuts." My voice goes up a few octaves. Erections in less than a year, correct? Nope, how about four to five years. Hmmm no erection until I'm 74 wowza that concept surely wouldn't stand (pun intended).

And by the way, while freezing your prostate kills the cancer, there's no guarantee so if it comes back my surgeon said he can do what's called a salvage operation, A mulligan of sorts.

After an hour of reviewing the MRI results, the pros and cons of the various options I/we made the decision to exorcise my prostate via da Vinci robotic prostate surgery. Radiation was to be held in reserve and only used if necessary downstream. I'm salvageable!

Surgery was scheduled for Thursday August 30th, 2018 at 7:00 a.m., with check in at 5:30 a.m. (90 minutes ahead, just like the airport).

26
A Radical Course: Prostatectomy - Robotic Surgery

All the world's a stage,
And all the men and women merely players;
They have their exits and their entrances;
And one man in his time plays many parts.
- William Shakespeare, *As You Like It*

Here's the play-by-play narrative.-

Surgery: You can't make this stuff up!

We checked into a nearby hotel the night before surgery since we lived an hour drive from the hospital. My evening was spent doing bowel preparation. I will skip the details but it wasn't a romantic evening.

At 5:30 a.m., I reported for surgery and was ushered into a private room to disrobe and don a stylish hospital gown. Surgery was set for 7:00 a.m., but the anesthesiologist ("happy juice") arrived 45 minutes late.

Thoughts of him being on a bender or just having made bail raced through my mind as I was wheeled into the surgical suite nodding off to dreamland.

What follows is the transcript of my surgery. If you want a visual you can see one at the USMD Cancer Center website www.usmdpcc.com.

Operative Indications:

* *This patient has biopsy proven prostate cancer. He has been advised of all of the treatment options for clinically localized prostate cancer and has agreed to undergo radical prostatectomy.*

* *He has specifically acknowledged the risks of incontinence, impotence, failure to remove all of the cancer, recurrence of the cancer, and the possibility of conversion to an open procedure and has given his consent to proceed with the surgery.*

I agreed to all of those potential outcomes? Holy Crap!

It is very important that you and your spouse have a clear head about the inherent risks in any surgical situation, but particularly one which has a major impact on a man's plumbing.

And, oh by the way, they didn't mention shrinkage? I know there are trade-offs like improved golf scores, or ascent to Pickleball champion, but at the expense of my pal Oscar?

Thank you Karen, for being my steadfast advocate and taking great, detailed notes so we could have an intelligent conversation with the doctors. It takes two to play.

Operative Technique
(the transcript of my surgeon's notes)

After the induction of anesthesia, the patient was placed in the modified trendelenburg position with the hips slightly abducted and pressure points carefully padded.

The abdomen and genitalia were carefully prepped and draped in a sterile fashion. A proper "time out" was performed. A 22 french foley catheter was placed into the urethra to drain the bladder, and connected to a closed drainage system.

A pneumoperitoneum was obtained in the standard fashion using the BTT trocar. The camera was introduced and the remaining ports were placed under direct vision.

Two 8mm robotic trocars were placed in the right lower quadrant. An 8mm robotic trocar was placed in the left lower quadrant.

A 12 mm bladeless trocar was placed laterally in the left lower quadrant. A 5mm port was then placed to the left of midline for the assistant.

The robot was docked to the robotic ports. The instruments were introduced.

The dissection was commenced by incising the peritoneum just lateral to the medial umbilical ligaments connecting these incisions as high as could be reached.

The space of Retzius was developed. (note: this is an area in the lower abdomen between the bladder and pubic bones.)

The prostate and endopelvic fascia were cleaned of superficial adipose tissue. The superficial dorsal venous complex was divided using bipolar energy and monopolar energy and the stapler.

The endopelvic fascia was then divided with scissors bilaterally. The levator muscles were pushed away from the lateral edge of the prostate. The puboprostatic ligaments were divided. The dorsal venous complex was then divided with the laparoscopic vascular stapler.Sliced, diced, and folded.

What?

The anterior bladder neck was then divided with monopolar cautery. The foley catheter was delivered through this incision and used as traction. The posterior bladder neck was divided and the vas deferens and seminal vesicles were individually dissected free and divided.

As these structures were pulled anteriorly, the rectum was dropped away from the prostate. The pedicles were dissected and divided to spare both neurovascular bundles.

The urethra was divided and the prostate was then freed. The prostate was placed in a laparoscopic entrapment sac.

The lymphatic tissue medial to the external iliac vein, lateral to the bladder, proximal to the pelvic sidewall, and distal to the bifurcation of the iliac vessels was excised on both sides of the bladder.

The tissue was submitted for permanent pathology. Hemostasis was obtained with cautery and hemoclips.

A two-layer stitch approximating Denovilliers' fascia to the rectourethralis muscles was then accomplished with 3-0 V Lock suture. The urethrovesical anastamosis was then completed. A double armed stitch of 3-0 V Lock suture was tied at the loose ends was used in a running fashion. The 20 French foley catheter was introduced, and the bladder was irrigated with no significant clots apparent.

The anastamosis was observed for leakage and none was seen. The catheter was placed to gravity drainage. Flo seal was placed along the pedicles and previously ligated dorsal venous complex to aid with hemostasis. Hemostasis was then noted at low abdominal pressure.

I then placed the 16 Fr SP tube under direct vision and a PDS suture was used to affix the bladder to the anterior abdominal wall.

The specimen was then retrieved via the midline port and the incision was widened slightly to admit the specimen. The fascia of the port site was closed with a interrupted 1 Vicryl suture.

The subcutaneous layer of all port sites was closed with interrupted 3-0 absorbable sutures. The skin was closed with Dermabond glue.

Did they use Super Glue on me?

The patient was taken to the recovery area in stable condition. Instrument and sponge counts were correct at the end of the case.

That's a relief. Thank God for sponge counts.

As I regained consciousness a nurse hovered over me and Karen was at my side. The first thing I noticed was that the back of my throat was scratchy and bone dry. Turns out the oxygen tube is the culprit. Then I peeked under my hospital gown.

Yikes, six incisions and an apparatus just below my belly button!

It looked like an oil well head. The dreaded Foley catheter was there as promised. I'm wheeled to my hospital room in a haze. "Purple Haze" by Jimi Hendrix wafted through my mind.

Let's review. The goal of da Vinci prostate surgery was to:

1) eliminate the cancer altogether assuming it was truly contained in the capsule (85% confidence)

2) check a lymph node packet for possible cancer cells. (done),

3) Maintain or improve the quality of my life which primarily meant little or no incontinence (done), and

4) restore erections by saving the nerve bundles around the prostate. (100% saved on one side, 80% on the other (done).

Moving forward, it's PSA/Testosterone tests to confirm a stable <0.01 undetectable result and that it's stable over time. The battle has been waged and we've reached a stalemate for now.

Now, where is Karen? I vaguely hear "Emergency in the lobby, emergency in the lobby."

I rolled my eyes and faded into a deep sleep. I never gave a thought that this involved my beautiful, in shape beautiful bride.

27
"Houston, We Have a Problem" (Karen Takes Flight)

An excellent wife is far more precious than jewels. The heart of her husband trusts in her, and he will have no lack of gain. She does him good, and not harm, all the days of her life.
- Proverbs 31:10

Yes she is…However…

Still hazy from the anesthesia I thanked the surgeon, the nurse, God, St. Joseph, St. Francis, my friends, neighbors and all of the ships at sea for their prayers and support. Most important my wife Karen who has put up with me for 46 years and was with me every step of the way until another major detour occurred which presented a new life challenge.

I'm on the way to recovery and everything is on schedule. Karen left me in ICU to meet up with Bill and Fran Hackley in the waiting room. Bill and Fran had surprised Karen with a supportive visit.

They headed downstairs to the first floor elevator and Karen "believing" she could fly took off from six to nine steps from the bottom landing on the marble floor below shattering her elbow, hitting her head rendering her unconscious with bruising. All I heard was "Medical Emergency in the Lobby" over the public address system. I had no clue what had just occurred and went back to sleep. I was clueless.

After a while, Bill and Fran walked into my room while Karen was in the emergency room. I asked where Karen was and they said she is having lunch.

It made sense to me so we indulged ourselves in idle chit chat and I thanked them for their support. They left my Rosary Beads and Scapular and headed home. Still clueless, I went back to sleep.

It seemed like the middle of the afternoon and a nurse wheeled Karen into the room dressed in a hospital gown, heavily medicated, head bruised, and her left arm in a sling. What the Fork? Well, Ollie look at the fine mess we've gotten ourselves into.

We were now patients, sharing a hospital room. Our car was in the parking lot and there was no way that Karen was driving home in her painkiller induced condition. Robson Ranch is nearly 50 miles to the north.

I laid there with my phone in hand calling my brother Skip (Houston) who happened to be in Buffalo, NY on business. He was upset to hear from me so late with a status report but even more upset after learning of Karen's plight. He told me to standby and hung up. A few minutes later he called back.

Our niece Francesca's fiance Jonathan was on the way and it would be about an hour. Karen babbled on about being able to drive since she was right handed.

This was truly comical. I'm laying on my back with a Foley catheter, bloated by the surgery's multiple incisions, and we're flipping coins (figuratively speaking) to see who is the caregiver. Well, it's a team sport, correct?

Karen ultimately had surgery two weeks later and the first night was one to forget. I'm exhausted, dragging around an external catheter bag and our neighbors bring Karen back from surgery. She looked like she'd been in a car crash.

We survived that night and many since. Her recovery was much worse than mine and perhaps contributed to my success as I didn't have time to think about some of the issues that affect prostate cancer patients. Remember, "Improvise, Adapt, and Overcome." It's a continuing theme.

We continue to chuckle about this misfortune because laughter is the true remedy for painful events.

You might ask how I got home the next day when I was discharged from the hospital? Tom and Jan Knox, our wonderful neighbor had driven down to Arlington bright and early the day before to sit with Karen while I was in surgery.

They dropped everything and drove down to Arlington again on Friday to drive our car back to Robson Ranch, and they sat with me until I was discharged.

In addition Tom and Jan then drove back to Fort Worth for dinner. Amazing folks. We thank these angels on earth every day.

Tom is a prostate cancer survivor who had da Vinci robotic surgery at the Mayo Clinic in Rochester, Minnesota two years prior. I consider him a mentor,coach, and a friend through this detour in life.

In early June, we were chatting and I mentioned my diagnosis and he shared his story with me including the incisions from daVinci surgery. We battered him with questions until he loaned us his copy of Dr. Patrick Walsh's book *How to Survive Prostate Cancer* until we could order the latest edition. Karen and I read it cover to cover at least three times, and it is a constant source of information.

Tom's prostate cancer was genetic so he opted for da Vinci robotic surgery in Chicago several years ago. He didn't have the benefit of the Suprapubic Catheter so he had to have the Foley Catheter for over a week.

A Texan with the drawl and all the howdy's , Y'alls, and I'm fixin to go eat some barbeque we laugh every time we see each other.

Jan, (Tom's wife), bless her heart, took to Karen like they've known each other a lifetime when it was only four or five months.

Jan drove her to her surgeons' appointments, and then outpatient surgery by one of the best elbow specialists in North Texas, Dr. Mitchell Fagelman representing Ortho-Texas on September 11th, 2018.

A three-hour surgery turned into a long day. Jan texted photos of the post-op work which looked more like a zipper had been installed on Karen's elbow. She had a plate and mesh held in place by drywall screws. It wasn't a pleasant sight.

Neither was Karen when she was brought home that evening. Here I was standing there and I literally couldn't do anything but trip over my catheter bag. Tom picked up the prescriptions and we settled Karen into a recliner in our living room.

I was speechless, dreading a long night. Needless to say, I got no sleep. Neither did Karen and we stared at one another droopy-eyed until the next morning.

Fortunately, I was on my feet and had my wits about me. We were quite a sight as neighbors dropped in to check on us and deliver meals.

Karen's recovery has been very slow as you would expect from a shattered elbow, bruised hand, nerve damage, and arthritic shoulder, with occupational and physical therapy two to three times a week. Karen exercises daily as getting back in shape is Job One for her.

Every day is Groundhog Day at our house, starting with hand exercises, then onto shoulder work. After yet another visit to her surgeon, following being "fired" by her physical therapist, something had to be done.

Fast forward five months. After a long meeting with her surgeon, Karen decided to undergo not one, but two additional surgeries: arthroscopic surgery on her shoulder, and removing the plate from her elbow. An overnight stay in the hospital which turned into two, then rigorous physical and occupational therapy were to follow. Otherwise, Karen's nickname will be Quasimodo.

On February 27, 2019 at 1130 a.m., we checked into Baylor Scott White, Frisco for an estimated four-hour surgery. Karen is a trooper but was clearly anxious to get this done and embark on an aggressive rehabilitation plan.

She didn't remember the first visit and the luxurious building. I must say that Baylor Scott White Hospital is one of the most modern and luxurious medical buildings I have ever seen. A lobby with a rotunda, warm Texas greetings, and a step by step process to the check in procedure. Complimentary meals for family too.

Karen was whisked off to pre-op and I was later ushered into her "holding suite". The nurse prepared her for surgery. Her surgeon, Dr. Fegelman, stopped in and briefed her on the procedures on her shoulder and elbow.

The anesthesiologist had called the night prior and reviewed what he would do to insure that she was out the entire time and that a nerve block would be used in her shoulder. Then she was wheeled into the operating room.

I grabbed lunch in the cafeteria and then hunkered down to work on my laptop and prepare for a couple of meetings for Thursday.

Waiting for Karen gave me pause to think and then it hits me. As a senior (in age) it's a terribly lonely, depressing, and helpless state we are in right now. The long-awaited getting old. Is this what we've earned in life?

After 46 years of being Gypsy Travelers, we have arrived at a way station in life that demands immediate attention. I truly understand what my late mother and father must have felt in their last 10-15 years of life.

Fortunately, we have a rock solid support system . My goddaughter Kelly Reitz sent videos of her amazing children Josey and Bode that brought immediate smiles to Karen. Texting, Facebook posts of support all helped to lessen the negative thoughts(aka depression) which are a demon which needs to be slain.

The staff updated me when surgery started, the progress, and finally when she was taken to recovery. Five hours later ,I was taken to meet with Dr. Fegelman who explained that the surgery was very successful.

However, for the last five months, she had been manufacturing scar tissue which had to be cleaned up and her shoulder was scoped to give her greater range of motion. He also repaired the nerve damage.

Unfortunately, this accident also triggered underlying arthritis that had complicated her previous recovery. We discussed next steps and he indicated that she "may" have to stay one additional night because he had done two surgeries. Physical and occupational therapy would be aggressive and begin immediately.

A continuous motion machine was brought in to keep her arm in motion. I looked at this creation from the era of thumb screws, and body stretching.It did have a fleece pad to rest the arm on. I wondered if turned on too aggressively would your arm fly off? Hmmm.

I finally headed home at 7:00 p.m. with a cold front bearing down on the DFW Metroplex. The temps were already in the low 30's and as Murphy's Law would have it, I needed gas. I headed for the northbound I-35 toll road travelling at light speed while the "slower" traffic moved like molasses. There was no traffic on the toll road so I made it north to a gas station 10 minutes from home, tanked up and raced to Robson Ranch through a freezing rain.

Thanks to Fran and Bill Hackley, who had prepared a feast for my dinner and left it in our refrigerator.

Toby, our cat, stared at me while I devoured it in a matter of minutes . A glass of wine, relax with Toby on my lap and off to bed.

At 4:30 a.m. I awoke to Toby crawling all over me trolling for treats and a kibble refill. I had a 7:00 a.m. meeting in Plano, about an hour drive through rush hour. I turned on the news and the entire Metroplex was under a freeze watch and there were accidents everywhere.

I rescheduled my meeting to 8:30 a.m. since the highways in North DFW were treated with brine and headed down I-35 South jumping on to Express Lanes. There was absolutely nobody on the entire stretch for miles until I had to jump off to catch the G.W. Bush Turnpike east to Plano.

I arrived at 8:25 a.m. for a very successful meeting. Meanwhile at 7:15 a.m. Dr. Fagelman visited Karen and advised she would be staying a second day/night and physical therapy would commence immediately. I drove the 25 minutes to Frisco and had lunch with Karen. Great service, great cuisine. It's a hospital, for God's sake, where's the Jello?

One of the key learnings from this entire experience is that we are now classified as seniors and have absolutely no clue on the steps to take to arrange post surgery care. Neither do surgeons. We run for the exits when the fire alarm sounds. We go to our tornado shelter when the siren wails.

We have a three day survival kit with extra food, water, and supplies. BUT, when the da Vinci klaxon rings out, Awooga, Awooga, "battle stations, this is not a drill." When physical maladies attack our bodies, our minds turn into a bucket of clabbered puke.

I say this in all seriousness. We have spent thousands of dollars on long term care insurance and really did not pay attention to the details of our Medicare Advantage Health Insurance plan.

This series of events forced us to figure it out on the fly, but it takes one of you with a clear mind to navigate or run the traps.

So, here's the magic decoder ring and hopefully it will save you and your loved ones time when implementing a home care plan.

1) Read your health insurance policy. If you are on Medicare Advantage then your home skilled and unskilled care is covered except the discharge order must refer you to a social worker in the hospital who will make a referral to a number of agencies.

I engaged Brightstar Home Care because they were a national organization (a franchise) and had good reviews. Second, their lead RN did the initial plan of care for our Long Term Health company Genworth.

2) "Not so fast El Guapo" (*The Three Amigos*). Where the process is clearly meant to confuse the patient is that nobody tells you that the discharging hospital does the referrals, not the surgeon who only orders skilled nursing, and physical or occupational therapy. He gives that to the discharge nurse/social worker to generate the paperwork to be faxed (it's 2019 who uses a FAX?) to get the process rolling.

3). If your surgery was outpatient surgery the discharge social worker doesn't come into play so you've got to be in your surgeon or physician assistant's face to do the referral. Meanwhile, in our case the first time around we were miserable. So contact an agency in advance to walk you through the process. Brightstar takes care of insurance approval and what's not approved was to be covered by our long term health care policy.

4), In the case of paying caregivers by the LTC company, always ask, (no demand) that you assign the benefits to the long term care insurance company.

Unskilled nursing requires a credit card payment and you have to submit the receipts to the LTC company. Normal reimbursement is two weeks or less.

Home care companies will tell you that their experience is 4-5 weeks which may or may not be true but if you assign the benefits, they should bill everything to the LTC company.

5) In the case of Medicare Advantage plans that is an automatic except for any copays.

6). Equipment rentals may or may not be totally covered. Our experience was that there was a copay of $150/month which blindsided us. We were saddled with out of pocket expenses for physical and occupational therapy, MRIs, and X-Rays . We are seeking insurance reimbursement.

The entire process is challenging but don't give up. In the strongest terms when you do your Wills and Power of Attorney documents with your attorney, also do a "drill" or train each other on the steps to take when a catastrophe strikes and Awooga, Awooga you are ready to man battle stations.

A special thanks to Karen's BFF Zita Benander in El Dorado Hills, CA. Zita in a sympathy move, stepped off her son's bathroom counter and crashed head first onto the floor the day after Karen's surgery. She broke her nose, tibia, and like Karen, other assorted body parts. Karen and Zita had the text lines going strong for several months.

Karen's recovery is off to a great start this time with in home physical and occupational therapy. By the time of this book's publication, Karen will be at 75% strength chomping at the bit for life back in the gym and some sense of normalcy.

Section IV

The Post-Game Show

28
Post-Op: the next 8 weeks and beyond

Start from wherever you are and with whatever you've got.
-Jim Rohn

A hospital room isn't a suite at the Marriott and I was connected to antibiotic drips and fluids. The upside was that I got to watch the Cleveland Browns play an exhibition game. The downside is that I couldn't jump up and down or scream for the love of God tackle somebody! But I digress.

The nurses ordered me on my feet that evening to parade the halls with IV drip and catheter bag on wheels with my naked butt hanging out of my fashionable hospital gown. The next morning I hauled my butt out the door and into hallways for 20 minutes. I began plotting my escape if my surgeon didn't show up soon.

Recovering from major surgery requires understanding and following the doctor's orders. After spending a sleepless night in the hospital, I was sent home with a Suprapubic catheter bag strapped to my leg and carrying a jumbo bag for overnight draining.

By the way, Nurse Gertha, as my surgeon called her, had the recreational privilege of removing my Foley catheter (you've probably learned that it's a different kind of pain.).

What a relief! My surgeon checked the incisions and asked important probing questions like "Have you passed gas ?" I quickly learned it's important to pass gas as a first step to taking a dump.

A *no* answer implies the surgeon connected the pipes incorrectly. A *yes* answer drew a relieved facial expression. Little did I know that by the next afternoon passing gas would be a very satisfying event. The sound of such flatulence cleared the room of my trusty cat Toby and the boom was heard on the other side of the house!

I swear that I heard windows rattle! Thank goodness Karen was down for the count with pain killers.

I had the two-page week-by-week checklist as my marching orders. It's a list of Dos and Don'ts. Pay close attention to the Don'ts like don't pick up any item weighing more than 15-20 pounds especially while the suprapubic catheter is in place. Liquid diets, one cup of coffee/day, non fat foods.

Since I was on Tylenol pain reliever w/codeine, a stool softener is necessary because of constipation. We'll skip the details but suffice it to say, the first dump was almost as satisfying as the flatulence heard round the world.

A nurse came to the house three days a week for the first two weeks to check on the incisions and insure that the catheter was not coming loose.

Five days after discharge, I was instructed to close off the catheter and test my plumbing.

All kinds of thoughts were running through my head. What if my plumbing didn't work, just dripped, or worse was painful?

Fortunately, after many prayers and deliberation I stood over the toilet searched desperately for my slightly shrunken "mushroom cap" and looked up at the heavens as a steady stream flowed. My next milestone was checked off.

I pulled on a pair of Depends underwear just in case, puffed out my chest and strutted into the living room. Karen was out cold so I had nobody here to share this milestone.

The next challenge was sleeping with no leaks. This is where mind over bladder comes into play. With the catheter removed my bladder was getting used to having more capacity but was also used to flowing directly into the bag. This was going to be a testament for the kegel exercises and the remaining muscle controlling urine flow.

For first few nights, I was up three to four times. I quickly figured out that I needed to cut back on liquids that had been increased while the catheter was in play. I stopped drinking liquids around 7:30 p.m. and found that I only got up once (around 1:00 a.m.).

By the third week I slept through the night with no interruptions. Eureka! I've been reborn!

More importantly, there was no sign of incontinence but I transitioned to a thin pad just in case. My surgeon recommended visits to the bathroom every one and a half to two hours but not to try to hold it racing to get there. Remember you had major surgery and still healing. Karen, albeit staggered by her injury and Toby our therapy cat, were both by my side.

At three weeks, I could drive and took over as Karen's personal Uber driver which helped test my bladder successfully.

At four weeks, I drove to Norman, Oklahoma for a Delta Kappa Epsilon Fraternity Reunion and Homecoming football game at OU. Boomer Sooner!

Two and half hours without an urge to pee! Of course as soon as I walked into the hotel I made a beeline for the rest room. I had to strategize the tailgate party and game; so no beer, just a water with lunch, pee before kickoff, halftime and post game. A lot of up and down cheering but again no leaks, runs, or errors! The drive home was uneventful too! Confidence was building.

Weeks four to eight were spent walking and preparing to return to the Pickleball Courts. I was assured that at eight weeks resuming "normal" recreational activities was fine.

You will read more about Pickleball in my chapter "Pickleball Redemption." Steve Williams, another ex Intel Golf Bum who lives in Dallas, invited me to play golf in Prosper, over an hour drive from my home. This was a bit of a challenge because I had one cup of coffee prior to the drive.

The mind is a funny thing: if you think about peeing, you will want to pee. The good news is I drove for over an hour through traffic and stopped a mile from the golf course to relieve myself.

The round of golf was fun. I only needed to find 3-4 trees and I still had terminal shit swing with the old tire iron. We grabbed a salad for lunch, no beer for me, a stop at the restroom and an uneventful ninety minute drive home in traffic. I was very pleased. Life's simple pleasures.

Three months from surgery I was scheduled for my first PSA/Testosterone lab work. Anxiously, I move on with life. Diet change, increase exercise with Pickleball, personal Uber driver for Karen's appointments, grocery shopping and errands. So far, I was pleased with my decision choosing radical surgery.

I do have some fatigue in the afternoons so a power nap is usually a good thing and I'm getting back to work supporting Muddy Gecko, an outsource marketing services firm.

On December 12, 2018, the nurse called from my surgeon's office. The results were <0.01 Undetectable and testosterone was normal. What a relief! In March 2019, another round of PSA tests resulted in <0.01, also known as undetectable.

I am now scheduled for another PSA test in six months. Following those results I'll be tested yearly. I am officially a prostate cancer survivor. Yahoo! My beautiful wife kissed me and embraced me in a passionate hug.

There's nothing that will tighten the old sphincter muscle like waiting for your PSA results. On March 18 my meeting with Dr. Bevan-Thomas went very well.

He's moving on from USMD to the newly established Urology Associates. I will transfer my records to his new office and remain his patient for the next couple of years.

29
Post-Surgery Diet: You are What You Eat

Which brings me to diet or what you can and cannot eat following surgery and recovery. Mostly liquids the first couple of weeks then protein added to broths and no spicy foods to agitate my bladder.

I must admit that as I grow stronger my penchant for healthy foods grows weaker. I haven't lost my love for fine red wines or scotch(occasionally), I still crave chocolate but in smaller servings, and unfortunately red meat is a rarity, although occasional smoked brisket or ribs satisfy my carnivorous desires.

We have committed to eat our way out of this dilemma so that the pantry and refrigerator/freezer only had healthy foods. Here's a list from WebMD and other sources that you should not have in your refrigerator. [20]

No, (and Never)
Lunch meats (other than sliced turkey)
Hot Dogs (say it isn't so)
Frozen French Fries
Pickles
Beer
Gourmet Ice Cream
Tonic Water
Mayo
Creamy Salad Dressings
Frozen Pizza

Yes
Whole Wheat Tortillas
Turkey
Salsa
Hummus
Eggs
Seltzer
100% Fruit Juice
Plain yogurt
Celery
Cabbage
Fresh pasta
Avocado
Berries
Kale
Arugula
Lettuce
Tomatoes
Mustard
Lemons or Lemon Juice
Chicken Breasts
Broccoli
Carrots

We aren't quite there yet on a full detox from all the bad foods, ketchup included.

My guidance is to make changes even small ones, to eliminate fat in your diet, increase vegetable consumption and reduce if not eliminate red meats.

Our pantry needs to be inventoried with a focus on getting rid of unhealthy foods like potato chips (OK, we have 50% less salt chips but they are rationed), cookies, candy, crackers (eat cruciferous veggies with your hummus), tortilla chips which have too much salt, (make your own), and replace out of date herbs/seasonings.

Make sure your seasonings are MSG free.

Constipation was another issue I've never really had to deal with. It's in an Italian's DNA to poop a Yule log daily. Surgery had my plumbing confused, so prune juice, and large amounts of fiber provided daily relief. Oatmeal, broccoli, apples, acorn squash, quinoa, black beans, almonds, and strawberries, just to name a few.

And one final prohibition: that daily cup of coffee (or two) no longer works. Damn!

30
Surgery Results

It's not over until it's over.
 --- Yogi Berra

One of the primary worries I had was that once my prostate was removed my Gleason score would be significantly higher as reported by a number of survivors on forums or literature.

The good news: my Gleason score was a 7 but a 3+4 grade group 2 (T2C) with a primary tumor that covered 15% of my prostate. The type of cancer was adenocarcinoma which arises in the cells of glands (ie. prostate).

The major worry was that my Gleason score would be much worse on final analysis following surgery. I have read many stories of men who went into surgery and the Gleason score on the extracted prostate was a nine or ten which increases the risk of distant metastasis. My final results were slightly better at a seven (3+4) versus the initial of 4+3 and my decision to excise the demon prostate was the correct call.

While a distant metastasis couldn't be addressed, all signs were positive: the cancer had not broken out of the prostate capsule. That also included the bladder neck, seminal vesicle, margins and the lymph node packets removed for analysis.

An excellent result was that my surgical margin was negative ie zero. Surgical margin up to 3.0 is a potential indicator of future recurrence.

I wasn't exactly elated when my surgeon informed me that he had an 85% confidence that I was totally cured. The reality is you are never "cured" with this beast.

Remember the goals of surviving prostate cancer. Radical prostate surgery and 85% confidence? This doesn't seem fair.

The battle wasn't over but a major skirmish has me in a good position on the battlefield. I am a survivor which means I will have to be tested every three months, then every six months, then yearly forever.

My remaining lifetime will involve a steady cadence of anxiety and worry while waiting for blood test results, hoping for a PSA score starting with multiple zeros.

Prostate cancer can re-emerge at some point and does according to statistics and anecdotal evidence. When it is detected, there are a few options most notably salvage radiation of different proportions.

The next milestones for me will be PSA/Testosterone tests. The anxiety will never end although a <0.01 PSA in December and March were a great relief.

I am officially a prostate cancer survivor …..for now.

It feels like playing Russian roulette with a revolver.

It's a source of depression, with thoughts of the cancer reemerging in the future. Diet and exercise are my only hope and there's no time like right now to make those changes.

31
Mind over Bladder

The mind is just like a muscle - the more you exercise it, the stronger it gets and the more it can expand.
— Idowu Koyenikan

Once you begin to take note of the things you are grateful for, you begin to lose sight of the things that you lack.
— Germany Kent

The evolution of da Vinci robotic surgery has resulted in a very high probability that you can minimize if not eliminate incontinence (which may require Depends briefs, or at best pads in your briefs).

I call it retraining my plumbing. The one remaining muscle must be trained all over again to control urination and bowel movements. Even men do Kegels.

One week after surgery the catheter is clamped and the first test is whether you can urinate through your penis. That is if you could find it. Remember the fine print about shrinkage. Oscar was now a mushroom cap. Once I was able to coax it out of its hiding place, I had a steady stream. Eureka!

The main issue was the large quantities of liquids taken to flush the system into the catheter bag needed to be reduced. If not, I would need to set up shop in the bathroom.

The second is that straining during bowel movements can cause a hernia. Stool softeners are required every evening. Taking a dump has new meaning. I pray that the robot connected the pipes to the right exit point.

Let's get back to mind over that pesky bladder. According to my surgeon, the risk of incontinence is very low and worst case 30% of patients wear a pad (not Depends briefs) for some period of time until normal urination control "resumes". 1% face incontinence. Pretty good odds, I think.

Night Moves
Everybody is different, so my goal was to manage my bladder by reducing caffeine intake, no sodas or wine. Water as needed but stopping liquid consumption by 7:30 p.m. - 8:00 p.m. each evening.

The hard part was adjusting or lowering consumption but it allowed my bladder to rest longer especially late at night. Mornings peeing like a fire hose has once again become a pleasurable experience. Is that Secretariat, the Triple Crown Winner, in the bathroom stall?

My goal was to be free of pads by New Years which would be four months from surgery. Each week I planned my activities whether sports, church, business, or shopping. On New Years Eve morning I shed the thin pad and it was a great achievement. Back in boxer shorts and swinging free! Life's simple pleasures!

Driving long distances was the another challenge. Adapting to this new challenge requires thought and planning. It's not like life before surgery. I have to take into account the amount of the liquid I consume, such as coffee, and definitely no carbonated beverages are allowed.

Generally I can now drive over two hours without a stop. Sitting for a long period does put pressure on my bladder. Kegels helped at the outset and I seem to have control of the one remaining muscle.

It's important to drink an ample amount of water but don't over do it. A quick swill of cool water after a Pickleball game is plenty but be sure to drink in response to the heat and physical activity.

32
Pickleball Redemption

Dink responsibly

According to Wikipedia, "Pickleball is a paddle sport that combines elements of badminton, tennis, and table tennis. Two or four players use solid paddles made of wood or composite materials to hit a perforated polymer ball, similar to a Wiffle Ball, over a net." [21]

Congressman Joel Pritchard, Barney McCallum, and Bill Bell invented the game of pickleball one summer afternoon in 1965 on Bainbridge Island, WA. It's a racket sport on a smaller court than a tennis court.

At the net there's an area called "the kitchen" a sort of minefield that players cannot enter unless the ball lands there. Only then after it bounces can you step into the kitchen and "dink" (soft hit) the ball back to your opponent.

New players are often chided by veterans "you're in the kitchen," and "get out of the kitchen." You lose the point or the serve if you are caught in the kitchen. It is very annoying, but a nuance of the sport. Tennis players who pick up the game seem to forget that the paddle and the ball are remarkably different than the slam, bam, thank you ma'am run around like a fool and hurt yourself game.

We should post signs that say "No Running" or "No serving like Andre Agassi" or slamming the ball at the net rather than dinking the ball in a choreographed dance of the pickleball players. It is a chess game for sure.

As a passionate pickleball player it's fun to watch players put the ball at their opponent's feet, dink into the kitchen, drive the ball down the rail (side) of the court away from their forearm or deploy backhand shots. Age and treachery always trump youth and skill.

OK, ok what's with the name? It's a simple explanation. The Pritchards had a cocker spaniel named Pickles, who became interested in this new game.

Whenever a ball would come his way, he would take the ball and run off with it, because you see, it was Pickle's ball. And that is how the game got its name. And the USA Pickleball Association is sticking to it.

 We live in a 55+ Retirement Community in North Texas known as Robson Ranch We moved here in 2016 to take advantage of the many activities like golf, cycling,"boot camp" in the gym, and long walks. I enjoy golf and swinging the old tire iron abusing my fragile ego.

I bought a golf cart and decorated it in all things Oklahoma Sooner. I christened it the "Thunder Cart". The weather doesn't cooperate so we have to tolerate high temperatures, humidity and high winds in the summer.

The fall improves as temperatures moderate, but it's just too cold in the winter to play golf. There is nothing like being diagnosed with prostate cancer and playing terrible golf in miserable conditions. Too much time to think about the cancer as well as feeling guilty about that great cigar and guffaws with the boys. What was this sport called Pickleball?

Robson Ranch sports a huge Pickleball Club and courts. It hosts regional and international tournaments. Rumor has it that by the time of publication of this book Robson Ranch will be declared the capital of Pickleball in Texas.

My wife and I saw an announcement for a Pickleball academy and it was free so Karen and I learned the sport of Pickleball. Shorter court, lower net, a paddle and a wiffle ball. No need to run and chase the ball like tennis and residents of all ages can play

Upon "graduation" we start on the bottom of the Pickleball food chain, the D Group. $150 paddle and new kicks and I'm ready to play! Those that aspire to move up the food chain can be qualified through shootouts and thus matriculated to the "C" Group. Challenge up to the "B" and "A" groups.

The first six months was really tough because frankly I was out of shape and every joint in my body hurt, but slowly I worked on my game and became one of two trash talkers in our group.

Generally my new found friend/trash talker and I won our unfair share of our games.

So what is the art of trash talking? It is a form of insult usually found in sports events allegedly used to insult the opponent, but in my case is used in a humorous spirit. It also took my mind off the diagnosis.

Trash talking has various styles. I love rock and roll music dating back to the 60's only with a twist. For example: "*Do* Stop Believing", or "Who let the dawgs out?", or "Jenny, I got your number, 867-5309."

Seriously, Ginny is a real player and damn was she good at the game. Unfortunately she's on injured reserve currently. If I'm playing an Oklahoma State University alum a rendition of "Boomer Sooner" the Oklahoma fight song emerges or "Did you go to OSU? I'll speak slower". Texas Tech "Guns Down" and of course the Texas Longhorn alumni and fans get their unfair share.

I was muffled this year since the short horns beat us in the Red River Rivalry. "For the Love of God tackle somebody" and other profanities are spewed out. OU got revenge in the Big 12 Championship. Horns Down! There is no political correctness in Pickleball."Horns Down!" I am also a passionate Cleveland Browns fan so howling at the moon, woof, woof is often an icebreaker during a heavily contested match.

Love 'dem dawgs!

In the Spring of 2018 I started playing two hours a day five to six days a week. In May following my diagnosis I increased to three to four hours a day starting at 6:00 a.m.. My group is comprised of men and women ages 55-79. Having been whipped by 74-year-old women (I swear they had to be in their early 50s') who mastered the games inspired me to work harder at getting better.

Sports are competitive, but they are also about fun and fellowship. I quickly learned that everybody here has one malady or another. I played with prostate cancer survivors. The sharing of their experiences had a positive effect and as players learned about my diagnosis all shared their support and prayers. There are players with two knee replacements. Another with both knees and a hip replacement. This is a very supportive group.

I played up until the day before my surgery August 30th. In eight weeks, I'd be back on the courts because I set a goal to do just that and assume my position as a premier trash talker eight weeks to the day I was back on the court for an hour, then two days later 2.5 hours but it took two days to recover. I am back.

I'm playing three to five days a week but it's weather dependent and until I build back my strength and agility, I'm taking it slower. I am looking forward to advancing to the "B" group this year but I love my "C" peeps. Trash talking has been shelved for the moment while I'm regaining my "form" but it won't be long.

Meanwhile, the hunter (trash talker) has become the prey. My buddy has been flapping his gums so I've had to up my game. A humbling experience. The near term solution was to take skills training classes to learn the correct way to play the game.

Joe Baker has several great videos about doubles strategy. It is important to learn how to "dink" responsibly and getting to the kitchen line to defend your court. However, not everybody takes such an interest and soon games devolve into playing opponents using the elbows and assholes strategy. Lots of arm waving, slamming the ball at the net which percentage wise is a bad shot as the ball hits into the net .

The paddle is a wonderful weapon but abused it will haunt you. However it is humorous, but I always am respectful. "I'm laughing with you, not at you." Then I walk back to the service line shaking my head.

I've also learned that my group of players is very supportive of my diagnosis, surgery, and recovery. It's not unusual to be asked "how I am doing" or "you look well, is everything back to normal", or "You are looking normal".

Of course, I look normal for a eunuch, ever so temporary. Of course I wasn't normal before I had surgery running to the restroom between games to pee but now it's really not normal. Or a rock hard erection became a string cheese.

So don't throw "new normal" at me. It's a new way of living the extension of my life's experience. Adjust with conditions.

Pickleball Rocks!

Say it with me. (To the tune of Cleveland Rocks)

Pickleball Rocks!

It's a sport designed for all ages but seniors can play deep into their 80's. You can progress at your own speed and generally everybody helps new players to enjoy the sport. Another benefit is while not wildly aerobic it does help your step count.

I averaged between 6,000 and 10,000 steps per day prior to surgery. In the winter months 6,000 is a real challenge but indoor play helps. As we used to say in the Ex-Intel Golf Bums group in California when you are down on yourself for a poor shot "Don't be so hard on yourself. We'll take care of that for you!"

In 2019 after the spring thaw I am back on the links flailing away at the little white ball. Pickleball, however occupies my mornings.. Don't get me wrong. I'm not selling my golf cart and clubs quite yet. That elusive hole-in-one is still worth chasing.

33
Building Your Army of Support

Walking with a friend in the dark is better than walking alone in the light.
- Helen Keller

No Man is a Failure Who has Friends.
- Clarence Oddbody from It's a Wonderful Life

A diagnosis of prostate cancer can put a man into a dark place emotionally.

My number one priority was to enroll or enlist family, friends, professional connections developed over decades, my parish priest, Knights of Columbus fellow Knights and my family to take this detour with me.

"No One Fights Alone" is our mantra
(Prostate Cancer Foundation)

I was surprised by the number of prostate cancer survivors I have met through this army of support. All around the world I connected with over a dozen survivors to understand how their experiences would help my journey.

Each helped fill in the questions I should be asking and assuring me that da Vinci robotic surgery was successful in every instant.

Family support is crucial. My brother Skip, his wife Wanda, my niece Francesca and her fiance Jonathan all played a part in this detour. My sister Susan rallied her prayer groups and sent daily meditations.

Cousins Sandy Pasquino Cooper, as well as Helen Smith connected me with Jim, her brother (and my cousin), who was battling prostate cancer in Hawaii.

All were cheering us on from the sidelines and encouraged the wearing of a Scapular while in the hospital and sent a St. Michael statue for my office.

The Jones family --Karen's clan were all supportive from Tom and Deana, to Jim, Jane, and Sara. Kathleen sent words of encouragement to Karen throughout her ordeal.

Jim and Tom , the "Grub Brothers" , a moniker from their fishing exploits made trips from Oklahoma to check on their lil' sis.. Aunt Carolina and of course Floretta, Karen's Mom were in constant contact.

I don't recall a time in the past 45 years that Flo called me on my cell phone. She will forever be remembered for telling Karen with the speaker on that "Bob better be taking good care of you or I'll kick his butt." Trust me she's 91 and 4'8". I quake in my boots thinking about that warning.

You don't want to get "Flo'd".

Appeal to a Higher Power
I am a cradle-to-grave Catholic and have have had the privilege as a gypsy traveler to attend Mass all over the country, England, France, Scotland, Mexico, Cozumel, and Italy too.

My last parish was Holy Trinity in El Dorado Hills, California which was founded in 1993 with Masses conducted in Silva Valley Elementary School (AKA "Donut" church to children because of the complementary donuts after Sunday Mass).

I was blessed to participate in the dedication of the new church which I dedicated a stained glass window to my parents. A St. Francis Statue and bench with roses on my 50th birthday were dedicated to both of our parents.

St. Mark's Catholic Church is a new parish in a fast growing area of Argyle and Denton, Texas. It's is my new spiritual home.

Over the first few years the parish built a campus with a large parish hall which acts as the church on weekends for services.

The hall has a full kitchen and the parish offices. In addition there is an education building. The next step is to build a church to complement the property and serve this vibrant, socially active parish.

Father George, who is originally from India, has been in Texas for 18 years and says he's learned to appreciate barbeque, the Dallas Cowboys, and mastered "howdy". Whenever I greet him with "howdy Father" he busts a laugh that cheers me up.

What I'm saying is my parish is my home for quiet reflection,and the celebration of Roman Catholic rituals/ seasons.The Oh-Dark Thirty Mass (7:00 a.m.) on Sunday is the Mass for early risers. I am always greeted warmly exchanging handshakes, occupying our "reserved" seats.

Over the years I've moved from the back of the church for a quick escape at the end of Mass to my current position midway ever creeping towards the front. It must be a senior thing because I notice most of the first four to six rows are occupied by older parishioners.

Maybe it's because they are hard of hearing, or they want to be closer to God. God Bless them. Mass for me is an opportunity to reset my spiritual being for the upcoming week. I am still a traditionalist preferring the Latin Masses of old, As a young altar boy I had to learn all of the Mass responses in Latin.

Even now when the priest says "Peace be with you" I think Dominus Vobiscum. When the congregation responds "And with your spirit", I think "Et cum spiritu tuo."

There have been so many changes since Vatican II that I just adapt to the changes. I have Father Tom Sawyer to thank for my dedication to Sunday Mass.

I met Tom when he was a seminarian in the Washington D.C area. I regret not keeping in touch over the years but his advice to me as I left for college was to remember that the Catholic Church is omnipresent , always there everywhere, and most important there for me. I have concluded that this was one of the biggest blessings of my life.

After Mass in May I corralled Pastor Father George for his blessing when I told him of the diagnosis and also a week prior to surgery. He blessed my Scapular to be with me during surgery along with my Rosary.

I am a Third Degree Knight in a very active Knights of Columbus organization supporting the parish community. I asked for their prayers and support and following surgery brother knight Tom Royster brought Holy Communion to our home for three Sundays. I really enjoyed our conversations following surgery on Sundays. The prayer shawl made by Tom's wife Shirley and the Prayer Shawl Group was given to Karen offering prayers of support for her speedy recovery. We thank them for their nimble fingers and prayers.

Karen is a member of The Spiritual Awareness Center. Just another path to the same heavenly doorway.

Enroll your Facebook Friends

I have over 762 Facebook friends. While there's a lot of concern these days about privacy, I threw caution to the wind and announced my diagnosis in May with updates leading up to surgery. Support from over 90 Facebook friends was overwhelming. The troops have been rallied!

ProstateCancer.net on Facebook is an excellent place to share experiences and ask questions. This isn't misery loves company but it is reassuring that you are not the only one with an issue.

I am a moderator on their Facebook page and I've contributed five articles to-date, which offer my uniquely irreverent take on my experience with prostate cancer. Health Union sponsors an array of forums for specific diseases or conditions. www.health-union.com.

The Prostate Cancer Foundation also has a Facebook page and forum. They also publish reference brochures that can be downloaded.

Create your own Facebook group to share your experience.

Enroll College Fraternity Brothers

Delta Kappa Epsilon (DEKE)
From the Heart Friends Forever (DEKE Motto)

The most influential associations I have made were with my Deke fraternity brothers. It took over 40 years to reconnect with them and every day I get a text, email, or Facebook comment from one of my brothers. We crossed paths with several brothers (Ron Sorter, Fred Streb, Bill Nation) at various points in our lives.

Delta Kappa Epsilon was founded 175 years ago in 1844 at Yale. There have been many famous Dekes over the years. Notably Presidents Teddy Roosevelt, Rutherford B. Hayes the late George H.W. Bush, George W. Bush, and Gerald Ford. Astronaut Alan Bean (4th man on the moon), Dale Chihuly , glass artist, Melvil Dewey (Dewey Decimal System), and the late Southwest Airlines founder Herb Kelleher (A Texas Deke).

In the spring of 1968, I pledged at the Rho Lambda Chapter of Delta Kappa Epsilon at Oklahoma University and moved into the fraternity house the fall semester. Admittedly a bold move for a guy who barely got accepted to college following an less than an illustrious run in high school graduating with a 2.2 GPA.

I studied hard my freshman year forgoing beer, women, and song. The result was a 2.5 GPA . Fraternity life was like the movie *Animal House*, but experiencing the friendships and bonds that last a lifetime is priceless. My roommate Bill Nation met his late wife Karleen through our Deke sweetheart group.

I married my Deke sweetheart Karen and of course there was our housemother, Mom Moran, who trained us in all things genteel. Our chapter's famous Dekes were Larry Wade(deceased), then-editor of the Elk City newspaper, and a famous alum who flew in for every home game from New York: Max Weitzenhoffer, a Tony Award-winning producer in New York and London. He was named one of six Oklahoma Living Treasures in 2006.

Brother Wayne Hughes and I spent the summer of 1969 at Fort Benning, GA, doing basic training for the Army ROTC program in response to pending draft notices.

The parties were as advertised, such as the graveyard party every Halloween. Hanging "Hank Helton" over the lunch hour on the big tree in front of the house was good for a scream or two along with the gravestones of the most unpopular school administrators and deans.

When I established the Student Services Grocery Store, Brother Bill Nation was our CFO/Accountant, and Fred Streb was our construction superintendent. Our pinmates Karen and Karleen helped with the initial ordering and stocking.

Fast forward 47 years, yes 47 years! I sheepishly admit that I didn't keep in touch with more of my brothers over the years. In 2014, a core group of Oklahoma University Rho Lambda chapter Deke alumni brothers started hosting a reunion during the University of Oklahoma homecoming weekend.

Keep in mind that it been over 40 years since we tipped a beer together.Some things never change. The tales of years past get larger in scope, funnier by the word, and yes we've all put on some poundage. Dang!

Maybe it's the timing but it's great to have my brother DEKE's supporting this fight. It's been said that there are good friends and there are fast friends. A fraternity brother is a great friend because as we met again it was almost like yesterday. George Otey, an attorney from Tulsa (who would have thought it?) drove the creation of a new chapter at Oklahoma State.

By the way, our house folded in 1972-3. My sense is that most of us were from out of state and not enough in state membership to keep the house alive. It was also a time where fraternities were losing popularity. Larger houses were likely to survive with strong alumni support legacy and pledge classes. Small houses were doomed.

Over the years our house was sold and a small fraternity gave it a go, then the University bought the property and a shiny new building was erected dedicated to a deep pocketed alumni with no evidence of our existence. Not even a plaque. Our annual homecoming reunion is held on the grounds of 700 Elm which is appropriate. On the plus side, there was no social media or smartphones, just Party Pix or Kodak cameras with film that had to be developed.

Maybe even a Polaroid camera taking instant pictures. Good thing, but in today's environment we would all be tarred and feathered tarred and feathered for getting shit-faced (versus black face which never happened in our house). We have our yearbooks, pictures, and memories of our time at OU. Nobody can take that away.

So why you might ask this rant? A man's life's connections and influencers start with their parents, teachers, and in college my fraternity experience.

When I was diagnosed with prostate cancer I reached out to all of them for support. Of course I got needled (versus a rectal), but everyone rallied to my "cause".

I was determined to make the 2018 reunion aka The DEKE Roundup in late October. Bill Nation made his annual trek from Memphis to Dallas to spend several days with us drinking very good scotch and playing golf. We motored to the roundup and had a terrific time.

Several of the guys shared their brother's experience with prostate cancer and everybody shared their age driven maladies. We were still jolly good fellows but technology assisted with hip and knee replacements, shoulder surgeries and heart monitors.

Reenergizing these relationships has been awesome. From the heart friends forever.

Enlist your Ex-Intel Golf Bums (or whatever sport you play.)

As a golfer I may have terminal shit swing but I love to play golf especially with the EX-Intel Golf Bums. Many of us were in field sales, marketing, marketing, manufacturing and even IT.

These guys are ruthless in their relentless ribbing, but it's best to let them be hard on you than self inflicted punishment for a poor shot or missed putt.

The Ex-Intel Golfbums are a Northern California-based bunch of former Intel Corporation employees who have nothing better to do with our time so we play golf.

Founded around 2000 by a group of retirees from the largest above-ground salt mine in the world, a weekly game is coordinated by a member at various courses around Northern California. The bums now have over 100 members all over the country who flock to Lake Tahoe for our annual three day golf tournament. Golf is secondary to the relationships revisited and great wine.

Over the years, there have been trips scheduled to Phoenix, Bandon Dunes, Oregon, Half Moon Bay, Florida, Ireland, and Canada. In addition the highlight of my memories was our trip to Scotland. What a trip! Check out www.golfbums.org

Many of the bums reached out and posted on Facebook or email to offer support. Thanks to all of you.

Enroll your Linkedin Connections
My professional connections were next. I have over 2,000 connections cultivated since 2007. They all received the news too! Several business associates contacted me about their journey with prostate cancer and others referred me to their friends who have made the journey.

Write a blog/article or two about your experience. By the time this book is published I will have posted four or more articles on linkedin. If you aren't on Linkedin and are retired for example, create a Facebook page, use twitter, and instagram.

Enroll your Neighbors - Belvedere Drive Rocks!
Harry S. Truman said, "In order to have good neighbors, we must also be good neighbors."

Living in Robson Ranch, a 55+ retirement community, you can get desensitized to the size of the male population dealing with prostate cancer.

On one hand, it's easy to deal with the diagnosis. On the other hand I can empathize for those out in the "real " world with their loneliness and depression. Start with your friends in the community, your church, and if still working your associates.

It didn't take long and my army of support was growing and I was uplifted by the prayers, words of encouragement, and love especially by Karen, my wife (aka the saint).

We have lived all over this country and have been blessed with neighbors helping neighbors. However, you must be a good neighbor too. Moving into a retirement community implies that residents are caring as well.

When we moved into our home on Belvedere Drive our neighbors really stepped up for us. Joyce our neighbor walked across the street and welcomed us. Joyce took Karen to the Belvedere Babes monthly women's lunch. She is now officially a Belvedere Babe. Joyce is a widow who was preparing to move to a new senior condominium in Fort Worth.

She is a joy and when she needed help we were happy to lend a hand. This was taught to us by our parents who were always willing to help a neighbor. After Joyce moved she invited us to join her for lunch at her new home and brought flowers when she heard about our situation.

Tom and Jan who moved into Joyce's house were there for us and sat with Karen while I was in surgery. Jan drove Karen to her appointments and surgery. Tom and Jan made the trip to Arlington to get me home in our car Friday after surgery.

Tom is the prostate cancer survivor who introduced me to the book by Dr. Patrick Walsh, *Guide to Surviving Prostate Cancer,* and shared his experience with me and coached me (yes, I'm coachable) every step of the way.

Linda Smith, our next door neighbor, took Karen to her primary doctor the day after the accident and to Walmart for groceries.

Linda runs a thrift store in Justin, and made a special trip to the store in order find blouses with no sleeves because of Karen's cast. Linda stopped by and talked to Karen when she needed the conversation to take her mind off the pain.

At one point in the conversation I recall the two talking about healthy foods. Linda's husband Dell had open heart surgery recently, but his favorite vegetable was bologna. I almost fell off my chair laughing.

The next morning I was across the street chewing the fat with Tom Knox when Karen emerged from the garage in her hospital gown and robe.

Shocked, I walked up to her and asked where she was going. "I'm off to see Dell about bologna." It must have been the painkillers. I escorted her back into our home. That was good for a few chuckles.

The Belvedere Babes have a system called the food train. It's an app online where neighbors sign up for dinner meals to be delivered at 5:00 p.m. each day. What a relief. For the first two weeks, preparing meals was not one of our priorities. Linda Smith set this up. She is an angel amongst us.

Karen's workout and exercise buddy Maddi Dudley, brought homemade chili and delicious meals from Boston Market several times. We are very blessed and lucky to have such special friends.

I have been very fortunate to meet fellow survivors not only here at Robson Ranch but also around the country and as far away as China. Every survivor I have met wants to talk about their experience and we all get a few chuckles too. We are a unique men's club that admits only one out of nine men regardless of age.

Once you've enrolled your "army" in your fight it's incumbent upon you to lead. There's a U.S. Army Infantry axiom "Lead, Follow, or Get out of the Way". You have no choice but to lead so provide timely updates via your social media platforms, annual Christmas letter, blogs, and of course personal calls about your status good or bad. Nobody fights alone. Your "army" wants, no *needs*, to know how you are doing moving you through the eye of the needle.,

34
Financial Planning and Simplifying Your Life - Get Your House in Order

Bills travel through the mail at twice the speed of checks.
— Steven Wright

Rocky, my late father used to say "there's only two truths in life ---- Death and taxes." I beg to differ Pop! There's another constant in life ----- bills.

Upon learning of my diagnosis it was imperative that I insured that bills were paid through two months following surgery. This was in the event of unforeseen circumstances in my case. This was a fortuitous move because of Karen's unsuccessful flight off the hospital staircase because she would be physically and mentally unable to pay the bills.

Fortunately, I had my mind intact as well as both hands, so access to a computer was easy. If there is one mental benefit of this diagnosis it was clarity of mind. My penchant for research was sharper than ever. The time had come to simplify our life.

Pre-Surgery Financial Preparations
A month before surgery I set up auto pay on all bills by date due and the day prior to surgery scheduled the remaining through the month of September. We set cash and checks aside for paying neighbors for the prescriptions they picked up for us.

As I sailed through surgery and Karen underwent hers, we were able to recover without worrying that one bill or another would be due. Our neighbors brought in the mail each day and I quickly reviewed for bills, set them up for payment and filed the junk mail in the round bin.

By the end of September I set up payments again and now have a system for paying bills for the future. You might have noticed that I haven't discussed the "D" word (death) which is difficult but since we have our Wills, Trust, and Durable Powers of Attorney we will focus on final instructions in 2019 then put them back in our safe.

This got really serious when it was decided that Karen needed a second surgery on her elbow and arthroscopic surgery on her shoulder. Karen was going to be out of commission yet again.

Long Term Care Insurance
If you are in your late 40's or early 50's, I highly recommend Long Term Care insurance. This industry has been going through a huge sea change as subscribers are living longer and not dropping out thus premiums continue to increase.

Genworth is our long term care insurance company and has been well worth the investment. I strongly recommend that you read the benefits as if you needed them today so you clearly know how it works.

For example, we thought we had to continue premiums for Karen while being reimbursed for authorized expenses during the life of the claim. Since home care was involved there is no limit to authorized reimbursable benefits. This included grab bars in the shower and bathroom, new adjustable shower unit, bed rail, and shower bench. A local handyman came to our aid and installed everything .

In addition, once a plan of care is approved and ordered by the doctor/surgeon pick a well known care agency. While you can assign the benefit payments to them, this is only after a small reserve cash account helped pay for the reimbursable expenses.

However, after nearly 20 years with Genworth, they-raised our premiums 80% stating that it had nothing to do with our health, current conditions, or age. It was because policy holders were living longer , and wait for it…..forecasted cancellations didn't happen so Genworth is under financial pressure to support their policyholders. They have offered a series of options which are currently under review. The timing could not be worse.

Life Insurance
Review your life insurance with your agent and clearly understand whether you and your family are carrying enough insurance in the event you disappear into the ether.

If you are in your in your 40s or early 50s, you should clearly understand what you have and if there are conversion dates on term insurance policies, so that you can take advantage of rates and adjust your policies.

Unfortunately, one of my conversion dates lapsed so I was looking at the end of a 15-year term in 2020.

If I kept the policy, the rate goes up exponentially ($385.00/quarter to $1000/quarter) and the other policy lapses in 2023 with the same result.

Run the insurance calculators provided by the insurance companies online and you'll probably find that you were over insured especially because in our case our move to Texas resulted in lower home cost (almost double in California) .

With a conversion clause there is no medical examination required so don't let that conversion date lapse.

The elephant in the room is your survival rate based upon having prostate cancer so if you are told you have a 99% survival rate for 10 years and slightly less for 15 years the end of your runway gets very clear.

Of course, other maladies or accidents may occur so only God knows when it's your time. *Carpe diem* when it comes to financial preparedness.

Don't believe the ads for life insurance that claim "nobody is turned down for medical conditions.".

Don't believe any ads claiming "all applications accepted regardless of medical condition." They are just a hook for finding more expensive coverage. Another word for them is a hoax, a very bad hoax. I was turned down because I had a "history of cancer."

What we learned is that it is impossible to plan for the worst and the worst case happened. We were both incapacitated although I had my mental capacity to log-on to our Long Term Health Care accounts and start the process for Karen. My situation didn't require home care.

Here's the rub though.

If we both are really incapacitated we didn't have anybody assigned to pick up the phone or logon to our accounts to get the process started. Powers of Attorney (POA) need to be executed by the closest relative which is usually the person who'll manage your estate. Leave instructions which explain who to contact and the method so they can transmit the POA.

Even if you don't have Long Term Care Insurance my recommendation is to have a reserve account for medical expenses and safety upgrades. Each year add to this account. If you are 65 or older start installing safety devices, and rethink throw rugs.

Also, you should have your list of prescriptions in a easily reached space. Here in Denton we have our list in an Rx bottle in the refrigerator with a decal at the front door letting emergency services know where to find them.

If your family is nearby (like your siblings), ask if they can come and assist if needed. Even some of our friends from California and Tennessee made the offer unilaterally.

My final word of advice with regard to financial planning is to remove all worries prior to surgery and focus on a successful recovery the first two to three months following surgery.

Simplify Your Home and Surroundings
If there was anything we learned from settling my parent's estate it was that more is not better when it comes to personal property.

We have made numerous attempts at "downsizing" including when we moved to Texas. It still astounds me that we still have a lot of stuff. We discovered *The Life-Changing Magic of Tidying Up, the Japanese Art of Decluttering and Organizing* by Marie Kondo.

Marie also has a YouTube videos and a Netflix series which shows you how to make your life a lot simpler. This KonMari Method TM is an outstanding method of organizing your living spaces category by category. [22]

To be clear, this is a post-surgery strategy. Nothing should interfere with your recovery.

This is a mentally grueling activity because it challenged Karen and I to decide on whether an article of clothing, a book, even accessories "spark your joy".

We started with our closet of shoes and clothing, moved on to our office, kitchen, and are looking forward to warmer weather to finish the garage. Books were donated to our local library opening up valuable space on our shelves. There were four to six garbage bags of paper retained for absolutely no reason. There were two full bags of shredded outdated confidential documents.

By the end of the first quarter 2019 we will have freed up more space and kept only the things that spark joy in our lives. When Spring arrives we'll tackle the garage one more time. That's the plan.

It's like starting over which is a by-product of prostate surgery, renewed energy and life. Although it's like rewinding our life as things disappear.

Section V

Survivor Stories

35
Survivors

It's not a club I thought I'd ever join, but here they are, my new fraternity brothers: Gamma Delta Prostate. No, there's not a secret handshake, but there is a kind of shorthand of language and experience, of pledging and initiation rites, of lifelong bonding and brotherhood:

What was your PSA?

How was your annual Digital Rectal Exam Date with your urologist?

What was your Gleason Score?

How old were you when diagnosed?

What gave you more pain, your Urologist's arrogance or his needles?

Who did your surgery?

Are you wearing boxers, Depends, or going commando today?

If you are a male age 40-70, and you chose to ignore a PSA score of a 4 or above, or don't get annual physicals, you can't come in the clubhouse or help us tap the keg. If your mantra is "ignorance is bliss," we're going to "black ball" you from membership (ha ha).

I didn't take this journey on my own, and I'm certainly not going to put out an authoritative prostate cancer book on my own either. What you are about to read next is what I consider the apogee, the high point, a gathering of nine men (a full baseball roster) who have agreed to share their prostate cancer journey stories with you.

Don't take my word for it.

36
The Terry Talk

Author note: You've heard of Ted Talks, right? "Terry" is a prostate cancer survivor who graciously shared his story with me in the first-person, to widen the scope of experience, insight and wisdom in this book.

I was 48 years old when I had my first PSA test. I was never good at taking tests in high school or in college. At the age of 48, I was still not good at taking test and I failed my first, and only, PSA test.

My PSA was 3. This being my first PSA test, I had no concept of what a "3" actually meant. My general practitioner referred me to a urologist and the urologist immediately ordered a biopsy. Within two weeks of having my first PSA test, I was diagnosed with prostate cancer. There was no "wait and see" about it.

I spoke to as many people as possible. My mom is a breast cancer survivor and her oncologist is a prostate cancer survivor, who had written a book on prostate cancer. He agreed to meet with me and share his experience.

A friend connected me with a friend of his who had recently been through the same prostate cancer surgery I was about to experience. He became my prostate cancer mentor. We spoke multiple times throughout my process of researching treatments, as well as after my surgery.

I ultimately decided to have the da Vinci robotic-assisted radical laparoscopic prostatectomy. There were multiple factors that led me to that decision: I was fairly young and in good shape and felt it best to have surgery and remove my prostate to minimize the chance of the cancer breaching my prostate. Part of that decision was based on the volume of cancer that was found in my biopsy.

It was very meaningful to have the support of my wife who helped me through the physical aspects of post-surgery recovery. I found it very important to have support from men who were prostate cancer survivors.

First, I spoke to a handful of men who had chosen a variety of treatment options to hear why they chose their particular treatment options and how they were doing now. However, once I chose to have surgery I had one support person who had been through the same surgery and provided invaluable guidance throughout the months prior to surgery and through my recovery.

As for the future, my outlook is very positive. I am eight years cancer-free. I still have annual PSA tests that continue to be unremarkable with PSA scores less < 0.1

For men in who are in their 40's ,50's, 60's, I would certainly suggest that they begin getting PSA tests early on in order to establish a baseline. I would also recommend that they not panic if they do get diagnosed with prostate cancer.

If so, spend a lot of time researching before deciding on a treatment plan. If they choose surgery, I would suggest they make sure to choose a surgeon has performed a lot (thousands) of robotic prostate surgeries.

I would say that my life has not changed dramatically since having my prostate removed due to cancer. I now have to be more conscious about urinating more often and not waiting too long to find a restroom when I am out in public.

The surgery has impacted my sex life, to some extent, in a negative way. It has not been a dramatic change, but I would be lying if I said that it had no impact.

I agree with you, Bob, on the importance of humor. I can laugh about it now, but it was a very humbling experience having to wear adult diapers in the first few days after the doctor removed my catheter.

How is this for irony? I attended my granddaughter's 2nd birthday party and we were both wearing diapers!

37
Ray and the Robot

Author Note: "Ray" is another prostate cancer survivor who graciously agreed to share his story in the first-person to enhance the book..

I was 60 years old when first diagnosed with an elevated PSA, and the same age when diagnosed with prostate cancer.

My PSA had been between 1.2 and 2.0 for 12 years. Then it jumped to 2.9 and a few months later 4.3. That was early 2009. After the biopsy confirmed that the cancer existed, I scheduled my robotic surgery for mid-March, 2009. I decided in early 2009, after the 4.3, that surgery was the preferred alternative.

I talked to a close friend who had his prostate removed a few years earlier with the traditional (cut-open) surgery and his input was very helpful.

I chose robotic removal over radiation or "watchful waiting". Radiation has progressed over the last 10 years since my diagnosis and I understand it's now more pin-pointed and accurate which results in less collateral damage in that area. The "watchful waiting" was not a viable option for me. If cancer exists in my body, I prefer to have it removed rather than having a ticking time bomb.

My support team included my wife, who was very supportive and helpful before, during and after the surgery.

Ten years have passed and the surgery seems like ancient history. I'll be 71 in a few months and I'm in very good physical and mental shape/condition.

One of my concerns is colon cancer since my father had it three different times and finally died at age 76 when the third occurrence leached into his liver. I started getting colonoscopies every three years when I was around 40 and now it's every 5 years.

For men in who in their 40's, 50's, 60's, I would suggest getting annual prostate checkups (PSA and digital) at age 50, or before 50 if there's a family history. An enlarged prostate is very common and prostate cancer is detectable, treatable and very survivable with early diagnosis.

My surgeon had done over 1,000 robotic prostate removal surgeries prior to mine and I was confident my surgery and recovery would be successful. After the operation I was released the next day and waited a week before returning to work. Fortunately, I did not have to wear pads after the first two days.

Bladder control has continued to be very good. E. D. has been very manageable. The surgeon did a good job preserving some nerves in that area and everything works at age 70+ with an assist from Cialis (miracle drug).

There was yet another upside from the surgery. With the pressure from a mildly enlarged prostate removed from my urinary tract, I was happy to find that I could hit the urinal at the office from 2-1/2 to 3 feet away. Plus, it only took a few seconds to empty the bladder rather than the usual starting, stopping and dripping. Life is good, we are very blessed.

38
Tomba

Contrary to what you might think, Tomba is not an island in the middle of the South Pacific. Tomba is a long-time friend and he happens to be a prostate cancer survivor.

Karen and I first met Tom and Jean Bolger in Fremont, CA around 1978, near the beginning of the Reagan Administration. You remember Ronald Reagan, don't you? Tom and Jean are both graduates of Cal Poly, San Luis Obispo. They asked me to be their daughter's Godfather ("da gawdfawder") while Jean was pregnant with Kelly.

We've been close friends through the years, "almost family," (although I don't claim them on my taxes). Kelly is married now and has two beautiful children, Josey and Bode, who are on a first name basis with da gawdfawder! Tomba and Jean live in Belmont, CA.

I recently probed (pun intended) Tomba about his prostate cancer and his answers were amazingly insightful for this book.

Tomba's numbers were off the charts. In 2016 he had a PSA of 8.3 up from 4.4. Following a biopsy, his Gleason score was a 7 (4+3). After interviewing several prostate cancer survivors and urologists, he decided that radical (robotic) surgery wasn't in the cards.

Tomba shared with me that his "objective was selecting a treatment that would be effective and ideally 'non-surgical' to minimize the side-effects." Tomba chose a combo pack of Radiation and Brachytherapy, and after six months, his PSA is down to 0.9.

The only things Tomba notices now is more frequent urination and occasional ED issues which he considers wildly acceptable when staring at the stark alternative.

A detectable PSA was anticipated, decreasing over time post-treatment. I couldn't live with the fact that the PSA still is detectable, but I'm delighted that my friend Tomba beat those high scores.

39
Dennis: Don't Rely Completely on the Biopsy Results

A century ago, Texas was known for its outlaws, bandits like John Wesley Hardin, the Newton Gang, and a lethal husband and wife pair you know as Bonnie & Clyde.

Nowadays, the Lone Star State is home to rogue characters like me and my buddy, Dennis, who is a refugee from Chicago. Go ahead, say it with me: "da Bears."

Dennis is a fellow Knight at the St. Mark's (Denton, TX) Knights of Columbus Council 12553. We first met after a council meeting several months ago and bonded over our daVinci surgery initiation. The "normal" Knights in the room looked at Dennis and I like we were nuts, cracking each other up. I definitely concur.

Dennis was first diagnosed with an elevated PSA at age 49 (an upwardly mobile 3.5), and six years later received his prostate cancer diagnosis.

Dennis shared that when his PSA hit 4, he downplayed it and rationalized the numbers but went to a urologist from that point on.

He was Steady Eddie for a few years, drifting between a 4.3 and 4.5, his new "normal". He didn't talk to anyone about his condition initially, except for his wife (something I could have predicted).

In 2015, Dennis had a biopsy, "just to be safe." The biopsy came back with atypical cells but not cancerous. When his PSA jumped to 6.0, he changed doctors. Following an MRI and a targeted biopsy, Dennis went straight to the radical robotic prostatectomy option.

"I wanted it dealt with immediately and completely," Dennis said. "Fortunately, a good friend had just done the same thing with the same doctor a couple of years prior. Based on my age, the radical surgery looked like the best option."

Dennis can't say enough about having support. "It's essential" he said, grateful for the close friend who had had the same surgery.

"My outlook is really good," Dennis told me. " I was diagnosed with a 2mm positive margin, which increases my risk of recurrence, but two years in the clear is a good sign." Note: Surgical Margin which is within 1mm of the surgical margin predicts a greater likelihood of recurrence. 3MM is baseline. My surgical margin was negative so the likelihood of recurrence is next to zero.

Dennis is equally direct with this advice: "Don't wait too long. Start at age 45. My buddy had his prostate removed at age 48. And keep getting your PSA checked. If it is elevated and rising, get an MRI along with a biopsy. And remember, a biopsy alone may not be conclusive, as I experienced a year and half before I ultimately had surgery."

Dennis shared that prostate cancer is always in the back of his mind. He's had an undetectable PSA for two years now, but it's always a concern.

He is not completely continent ("a couple of beers and I'm on my feet for a good stretch, I may leak…otherwise all good."). He says sexually, things are different, but certainly functional.

Maybe this is why Dennis and I have clicked, with a similar sense of humor. He was sitting on his patio with another prostate-less friend, sharing a beer and laughs two days after surgery. Because of his catheter, he didn't need to get up to urinate. You look for moments like that, as a survivor.

40
My Cousin (Not Named Vinny)

Author Note: My cousin is a prostate cancer survivor. He is retired from the U.S. Air Force and lives in Hawaii. It's a very complex case, but overall the outcome is positive.

My cousin was 52 years old when first diagnosed with an elevated PSA, in 2006. Seven years later, at age 59, he was diagnosed with prostate cancer.

This illustrates the point that there can be a time lag, so keep watching your PSA numbers and don't take your eye off the ball.

When my cousin's PSA number rose above a 4, he told me "I continued to be tested every year and read up on what the numbers might mean.

My doctor also conducted a digital probe every year with no concerns. And I didn't have any other symptoms usually associated with possible Prostate cancer. "

After several years, his PSA rose to an 8 and the doctor told him" there was a greater than 50 percent chance I had cancer. That got me to have a biopsy."

For a sounding board he spoke with his spouse and family, recalling "Once I realized I had cancer, I was ready to fight it the best I could."

His treatment was lengthy and complex, so I'll let him tell you about it in his words:

"I was receiving treatment through a Military Regional Medical Center because they had better care than I could receive anywhere else in Hawaii.

"My urologist, after diagnosing me with cancer, told me I had three options. Regular surgery, robotic surgery (which he favored as that is what he did) or radiation.

"After reading a lot of medical publications, especially by the American Cancer Institute, I asked him point blank if he thought I might have metastatic cancer, in the lymph nodes or bones. He stated 'no' because it wasn't noted in my tests, a MRI.

"I reminded him that I hadn't had an MRI. He then scheduled one. I received a call from the urologist after the MRI, saying they were concerned with something on my bones and wanted me to do further tests. I agreed to two different bone scans.

"Afterwards, they believed it hadn't reached my bones and therefore I had a choice of the method of treatment. I decided on the radiation because the surgeons were all so young and I didn't trust them.

"I consulted with the radiation oncologist and he noted we could start radiation anytime.

"I was also going to need to have androgen therapy (hormone) injections because the MRI showed signs of cancer in my lymph nodes, the first time I had heard this. I immediately called my urologist and said I was on my way to see him and he would see me or I would be seeing his Commander. He noted he missed the info in the MRI report.

"At this time I demanded a second opinion from a Major Cancer Institute on the mainland and had already contacted Johns Hopkins. The military agreed to pay all my expenses for travel and diagnosis.

"I selected Johns Hopkins because they had an evaluation process for Prostate Cancer patients in which they evaluate and determine the best courses of action for the individuals.

"After my evaluation, Johns Hopkins categorically stated I could not have surgery, because the cancer was probably in the lymph nodes. They agreed it was not in my bones.

In fact, they wanted to start my androgen therapy immediately. Armed with that data, I returned home and had my first injection that week and continued them for three years. Shortly thereafter I began my 45 radiation treatments."

My cousin understood the value of a support network: "my spouse had breast cancer 3 years earlier and I knew that support was important. My spouse, children, and golfing buddies were my support team."

His outlook for the future?

"Looking good," he told me, "with no after effects of radiation. My testosterone returned to normal six months after the end of my androgen therapy and my PSA levels are still negligible. My golf handicap increased by two strokes, but that could be age related."

His message to men in who are in their 40's ,50's and 60's is, "get your PSA every year along with other blood tests. If it is rising, have a biopsy. Best to catch it early."

"Here's how my life has changed," my cousin shared recently. "What I learned was to know your body and question everything doctors tell you. The Internet provides a great source of information.

"Arm yourself with knowledge anytime you are involved in a medical procedure, and ask questions until you are satisfied.

"That lesson learned paid off when I went for surgery on another issue and had to confront the anesthesiologist and surgeon on the method of anesthesia because of other medical issues. They don't always read all your medical history."

Humor runs in our family, as you might guess.

"Since I was taking androgen therapy," my cousin recalled, "I was medically castrated by the hormones. Besides the lack of sex appetite, it also gave me a lot of the same symptoms my wife was going through with menopause including hot and cold flashes and more significant emotions than normal. Eventually, our hot and cold flashes synched up and we could get to sleep easier."

41
TK

"TK" is a friend who lives nearby in my housing community. He was 61 years old when his doctor first detected an elevated PSA, and the same age when diagnosed with prostate cancer. Genetics may have played a role since his father had prostate cancer.

When his PSA number rose above an 4, he immediately had a biopsy even though nothing could be felt by more than one doctor with the direct rectal exam (DRE).

Fortunately, TK had a sounding board during his fight, recalling "I talked to a friend of mine who had prostate cancer a couple of years earlier. He was also a minister. I suppose he was the only one I knew at the time that had dealt with prostate cancer."

He looked at several treatment options, but ultimately chose surgery. He related to me that he "looked at radiation but decided that I would rather get it out of my body instead of wondering if the radiation had gotten it."

TK shared that he had a strong support team in place: "After word got out that I had prostate cancer, other survivors came out of the woodwork to tell me their story and give me advice. That was very meaningful." He marveled at "the support from people at work, my family and my wife."

TK believes he is cured of the cancer, adding, "I do have to deal with the side effects of the surgery but they are minor, especially in comparison to the cancer."

TK 's advice to men in who are in their 40's ,50's, 60's, is as follows: "Don't ignore this silent disease. Most men will probably have it so it is important to catch it early. You have to monitor your PSA and have the DRE on a regular basis.

"My PSA was elevated but not by a great amount. DRE revealed nothing. Biopsies indicated a Gleason score of 6. Several doctors told me I did not have to be in a hurry and could take a wait and see approach.

However, I had surgery as soon as I could. The pathology of the prostate showed a Gleason 9! Waiting could have been deadly. Evidently most of my cancer was on the "dark side" of the prostate."

TK's life has changed to some degree because of his prostate cancer: "I have to deal with the side effects of the surgery, erectile dysfunction and incontinence, but both are minor."

And of course, there has been humor and the predictable loss of modesty: "For the biopsy, I met my doctor and the nurse for the first time in a rather 'exposed' position over the exam table, which I'm sure you can imagine!

"And here's another one. A week after surgery on my follow up visit, the nurse just told me to drop my pants and get on the table. While she cradled my member in one hand, she injected water through the tube into my bladder. Then I had to stand up and pee it all out in front of her.

"All this while my wife was sitting four feet away. I'm not sure if you can use this one in your book, but it is the raw reality of how this all works out if you want to save your life."

42
The Other Bob: Two Decades Cancer-Free

"Bob" (not me) has been cancer free over 20 years.

He was 52 years old when first diagnosed with an elevated PSA and 53 when he was diagnosed with prostate cancer. When his PSA number rose above a 4, he chose to confront it directly. He spoke to a few close friends as a a sounding board.

Bob chose surgery as his treatment method, because it had the least chance of recurrence. His doctors were confident the cancer was contained within the prostate walls and had not spread. Fortunately, he had an extremely helpful support team.

The upshot? 21 years with no elevated PSA!

Bob's advice to men in who are in their 40's ,50's, 60's? "Don't delay getting PSA test!"

His life has not changed all that much since his surgery:

"I'm 73 now, I have no leaks, everything is pretty much normal, although what can be considered 'normal' after two decades? During surgery, they saved the nerve endings which aided sexual activity, for the first ten years at least. I've noticed a decline in the past decade. Within the last couple of years my bladder control has been more difficult."

43
Is There an Author in the House?

Ken Arthur is a Robson Ranch Pickleball player and author of two books, *Exeter* and *Sojourner*. Both books are very good fiction reads. But here's the reality story of his prostate cancer.

Ken was 50 when his PSA was first recognized as elevated, in 2002.

Then came the prostate cancer diagnosis, at age 52: "When my PSA was discovered to be higher than expected at age 50, my urologist continued to check it over the next two years.

Finally, it reached a point where a biopsy was logical. The procedure revealed cancer. This was a surprise because of my relatively young age and the fact that I had no symptoms."

Ken and his urologist constantly monitored the elevated PSA numbers: "There was no denial."

Ken turned to several friends for support "Remember, this is the early 2000's. Robotic surgery was brand new and there were only four machines in the entire country at the time. I had a friend who had received his prostatectomy robotically and he was a key source for me."

Robotic surgery was the only treatment option Ken considered, sharing with me, "The significantly shorter recovery time, minimal blood loss, magnified camera viewing which diminished the chances for nerve damage, and smaller incision scarring were the biggest factors in my decision process."

"My wife was my primary caregiver," Ken recalled. "She took one week off from work to help me post-surgery. After that time I was pretty capable of taking care of myself."

Ken has written an amazing sequel to this cancer story: "I am 14 years post surgery and still have my PSA checked annually. I feel totally confident that, after all these years of, there is virtually zero chance any prostate cancer cells have migrated to any other areas."

His advice to men in the prostate cancer age group is direct: "Pay no attention to recommendations that suggest you do not need to check your PSA at least annually. In your 40's get a baseline PSA check and then have follow up checks done as you approach age 50."

Life has not changed all that much for Ken. "I was very lucky with the two 'Big I' items, Ken shared. "I was incontinent for about a month and impotent for a few months. Neither of those common side-effects of the surgery have been any problem in the intervening years."

Modesty goes out the door for most prostate cancer survivors.

Survivors are always on the mend, sometimes with humorous results:

"During the first week post-surgery (when the catheter was still in), my wife and I went to a restaurant. I decided I could carry my 'bag' inside a canvas shopping bag and hide the tubing.

"My biggest concern during the meal was that I would forget the arrangement and try to leave the booth without first picking up the bag. That didn't happen, but it would have been both painful and pretty embarrassing."

44
Chris from Shanghai

Author Note: "Chris" is another prostate cancer survivor who graciously shared his story with me to help widen the scope of experience, insight, and wisdom in this book.

Chris lives and works in Shanghai. Chris was first diagnosed with an elevated PSA and diagnosed with prostate cancer at age 56. When his PSA number rose above a 4.0, he confronted it straight away.

When I asked about who he had talked to, Chris told me, "I talked to a work colleague and a friend, both who had been through the same thing and both of whom had a prostatectomy. For the colleague, it had been ten years earlier, and five years earlier for the friend."

Chris looked at several treatment options: "Being relatively young, with the prostate cancer in its very early stages, contained within the prostate, I took advantage of the huge advances in technology and techniques and had a Retzius sparing radical prostatectomy using the Da Vinci robot."

Fortunately, Chris had a support team. He shared with me recently, "I was lucky enough to have my Mum and sister look after me, both ex-nurses, as well as my wonderful wife, for the all important first six to eight weeks.

"I made the point of letting close friends know. Just having their well wishes and kind notes from time to time, plus the odd visit, helped me remain positive."

His outlook is optimistic. It's been twelve months since the surgery and his PSA tests are are all clear. Chris is tested every four to six months, and in his words, "as time goes by the future looks ever brighter."

Chris had this advice for men who are in their 40's ,50's, 60's: "Take the PSA as well as the traditional (rectal) finger test. Find a doctor or specialist who knows what they are looking for. Also, don't be frightened to address the cancer if you are still young (your 40's or 50's). Technology is amazing and the side effects of surgery are reduced nowadays. I was dry immediately and the old sexual function returned pretty much immediately. One point to underscore: use a surgeon who has done at least 50 surgeries a year and one that uses the latest techniques and technology."

Like many of us coping with a life-altering diagnosis, Chris looks for humor to lighten the moment. He told me about a work colleague, who, "in his recovery, tried the blue pill, which did not work too well, and the injection, which worked too well. He had to go to hospital in agony as his raging hard on would not subside!"

"My life has changed in a positive way," Chris added. "I am now more aware of my health - leaner, fitter and happier."

Postscript

The Curtain Rod: I Can Do This
(Or, What's Come Over Me?)

There's nothing like prostate cancer to reorder your priorities and establish clarity in daily life.

Chaos was my life and suddenly my mind has become focused quickly solving problems I used to pay some one else to install or repair.

For example, the key fob for my car has batteries. I have paid up to $20 each to have the battery replaced. I opened the fob and discovered the battery could be easily be replaced for free since I had one in my battery stock.

I wanted to install a thick backdrop curtain in my home office, to make things more professional during Zoom Video calls, instead of my cat on a pedestal or some cheap-o window blinds and Texas sunlight providing a white-out effect so you can't see my face. Before my prostate cancer, I would have hired someone to set up the curtain rod, drill the holes and hang the curtain (my part might have been buying the curtain).

But here's what's different now. I did the project myself and it looks like a pro worked on it; a really expensive pro.

I have tremendous confidence in myself to figure it out, no matter the project or the dilemma.

I'm much more diligent and tenacious than I used to be, and believe me I was pretty darn diligent and tenacious before my Gleason Score shot me into the Adios-The-Living-Into-My-70's Zone.

Now, every time I look at that curtain, I know what's supporting it. I figured it out, and I'm going to continue to figure things out, indefinitely.

Karen and I updated our Wills and Trust including the letter of instructions with specific bequests. This is all done and filed away. Party on!

Even my dietary habits are changing to more plant based foods and literally no red meat. Of course that will be saved for special occasions but slowly and surely I'm embracing dietary change.

The point is even old dawgs can change or learn new tricks. I've become an advocate and a first time author with this medical memoir. As my dad Rocky said "who would have thunk it?". I've written articles for Prostate-Cancer.net and am a moderator for their Facebook forums.

Frankly it took a very serious diagnosis to change the trajectory of my life.

Gratitude: 2018 in a Nutshell (Yes, that's a prostate joke)

2018 looks like a multi-car crash on an I-35 overpass in the rear-view mirror.

Automobiles, like life, keep on moving down the highway. Karen and I are recalling the events that caused a major detour in our lives, but we are also moving again on the express lanes. To quote Dave Barry who is also turning seventy " I don't have much time left……..If our lives were football games, we'd be at the two minute warning in the fourth quarter."

In one year, we both had a Cancer diagnosis, and I have suffered from hearing loss, ergo hearing aids. Karen has always accused me of "selective hearing" but this was the real thing. Say, what?

Karen, a.k.a. Saint Karen, shattered her elbow, suffered a concussion, damaged her shoulder and wrist. This is all on top of her Dystonia (neck tremors), a distant cousin of Parkinson's disease. Yes, this means Karen can easily friend Michael J. Fox on Facebook.

Our kitchen calendar is now populated with appointments with doctors, surgeons, occupational therapist, and specialists. Seriously, you just can't make this up.

Here's the play-by-play for 2018. Warning, there will be a test at the end, but it will be multiple choice.

The first quarter of 2018 saw me dealing with an elevating PSA, while Karen had a spot on her head which was diagnosed as skin cancer. After three PSA tests, my urologist scheduled a biopsy for May.

In the second quarter, Karen had a skin cancer removed and she's now cancer free. My biopsy results indicated prostate cancer. Early detection indicated that the cancer was slow growing and contained in the prostate.

We met with my urologist, Dr. Jaderlund, and Dr. Rich Bevan- Thomas a surgeon at the USMD Cancer Center in Arlington, Texas. There was a rock band in the 1960's called Three Dog Night; I guess I'm still looking for my third doc….

Karen was a terrific advocate and took great notes asking questions from the research we both were doing on treatment options. Following an MRI in June we met again with the Dr. Bevan-Thomas and decided on removing the prostate utilizing da Vinci robotic surgery scheduled for August 30th.

Glad you enjoyed the halftime show.

The third quarter of 2018 saw us making a trip to Breckenridge, Colorado in early August, knowing there were not going to be any long trips planned for the rest of the year. I had been playing Pickleball three hours a day since May so I was in pretty good shape for the surgery.

On August 30th, my prostate was removed successfully. Happiness turned to "shock and awful" when Karen fell down the marble stairs at the hospital and shattered her elbow, was knocked unconscious bruising her head and suffered a concussion. Imagine waking up with the entire emergency room staff hovering over you!

If you do have to fall, do it in a hospital! Two patients do not equal one caregiver. It was a shit show for a time.

Our niece's fiancé Jonathan drove to Arlington on short notice to take Karen home. We are blessed to have great neighbors who came to our rescue. Our neighbors Tom and Jan Knox picked me up when I was discharged from the hospital.

Tom and Jan also took us to our doctor appointments and Karen to her surgery. Picture Bob sporting an external catheter bag and Karen in a sling going into Labor Day weekend. This was a uniquely interesting time together. I haven't had this much fun since the pigs ate my brother (a Texas expression).

The first couple of nights following Karen's surgery were frightful. Thanks to Linda Smith, our neighbor who took Karen to the doctor and organized the neighborhood meal deliveries for the first two weeks by neighbors.

Maddi Dudley brought Boston Market meals too! Beautiful flower arrangements cheered us up from the Jones and Bolger/Reitz family.

An Edible fruit arrangement from Skip and Wanda Tierno arrived as well. Thanks!

Toby our "therapy cat" was our calming influence as he jumped into our laps purring us to sleep.

The fourth quarter saw Karen seeing an occupational and physical therapist three times a week. On December 3rd, Karen's surgeon identified additional damage to her hand, wrist, and shoulder. During the first quarter of 2019 Karen had a second surgery on her elbow and shoulder. She's still going to physical and occupational therapy making improvements daily. She can even put on her earrings!

I'm doing well in my recovery with no major issues. In September my surgeon was 85% confident that they removed the cancer. On December 6th I had my first PSA Test since surgery. On December 14th the results were <0.001 undetectable cancer free!

Fast forward, three months later in March of this year, and another PSA test result of <0.01 undetectable. Next test is in six months. I'm looking forward to high anxiety awaiting PSA results following blood tests.

We decided that this has to be "the worst" which we committed to in our marriage vows. We take one day at a time with lots of laughter between us. Well, most days, anyway.

But here's the upside. I have been rerouted to a new runway (yes, this is now a "Planes, Trains and Automobile" chapter), that offers 10-15 years of life with a new meaning including a new role as an advocate, moderator, and author.

Pickle Ball continues to best explain this new life. There may have been a few unforced errors on my part when addressing prostate issues. But staring down the line at my opponent, tied with a score of ten all, I have the yellow bola in my hand, preparing to deliver the match point.

I take a breath, briefly remembering the terror of the past year . The ball is served swiftly and deep. My opponent returns it directly back to me. Anticipating another deep return, I turn the tables and dink it into the kitchen impossible for my opponent to get it. Game over!

With this new found "win" beating prostate cancer I am motivated in so many ways as I approach my 70th birthday in June. The U.S. Open at Pebble Beach awaits!

Appendix

References

"Do you have references?" It's what you're usually asked during a job interview. So also for a book. I have been as precise as a da Vinci robot in listing the sources of supporting information for my book.

Introduction
1 "Solitude", Eli Wheeler May 25, 1883
2 American Cancer Society 2018 Report

Chapter 1
3 *The Emotions of Normal People*, William M. Marston, Persona Press, 1971 and "The Universal Language DISC", Target Training International, 2007

Chapter 3
4 "A Closer Look at Laughter Therapy," Cancer Treatment Centers of America https://www.helpguide.org/articles/mental-health/laughter-is-the-best-medicine.htm
5 "The Benefits of Laughter", CMN Alternative Cancer Treatment, December 27, 2016

Chapter 5
6 "Prostate Cancer, NCCN guidelines for Patients", Version 1, 2016 (National Comprehensive Cancer Network)
7 "Prostate Cancer Patient Guide", Prostate Cancer Foundation, 2019

8 "PDQ Cancer Information Summaries" National Institute of Health, Bethesda (MD): National Cancer Institute (US); 2002.
9 *Guide to Surviving Prostate Cancer*, Dr. Patrick Walsh and Janet Farrar Worthington, Fourth Edition 2018

Chapter 6
10 *Fortune*, May 13, 1996
11 *Andy Grove*, Richard S. Tedlow, 2006; Penguin Books

Chapter 13
12 *Finishing Strong*, Steve Farrar, Multnomah Books, 1995

Chapter 14
13
https://www.cancer.org/cancer/prostate-cancer/treating/by-stage.html

Chapter 15
14
https://www.mayoclinic.org/diseases-conditions/high-blood-pressure/in-depth/alpha-blockers/art-20044214

Chapter 16
15 Guide to Surviving Prostate Cancer, Dr. Patrick Walsh and Janet Farrar Worthington, Fourth Edition 2018

Chapter 18
16
https://en.wikipedia.org/wiki/Homeopathy

Chapter 19
17 https://www.ifm.org/functional-medicine/

Chapter 23
18 http://www.uant.com/urologic_oncology/cryosurgery-cancer-prostate-kidney.php

Chapter 24
19 Walsh, op. cit.

Chapter 29
20 https://www.webmd.com/diet/qa/what-can-you-eat-to-prevent-prostate-cancer

Chapter 32
21 https://en.wikipedia.org/wiki/Pickleball

Chapter 34
22 "The Life-Changing Magic of Tidying Up , the Japanese art of Decluttering and Organizing" Marie Kondo, Ten Speed Press 2019, translated from the Japanese by Cathy Hirano

Coming to Terms

66 Prostate Terms You Can Use Legally in Scrabble

Active Surveillance: in prostate cancer , this is the process of delaying definitive treatment until it becomes clear, through vigilant monitoring that the cancer is growing and on the move.

Alpha Blocker: According to the Mayo Clinic these medications relax the muscle in the prostate and bladder neck There are five medications such as terazosin (Hytrin), doxazosin (Cardura), tamsulosin (Flomax), alfuzosin (Uroxatral), and silodosin (Rapaflo).

Alternative Medicine: Alternative medicine describes any practice which aims to achieve the healing effects of medicine, but which lacks biological plausibility and is untested or untestable. In some cases AM treatments are proven ineffective. (source: Wikipedia)

ADT: See Hormone Therapy

Androgens: Male Hormones, also known as testosterone.

Artificial Urinary Sphincter: An implanted device to treat incontinence that has persisted for a year or longer and shows no signs of improving.

Benign: Not cancerous, not fatal

Biomarker: In medicine, a biomarker is a measurable indicator of the severity or presence of some disease state. More generally a biomarker is anything that can be used as an indicator of a particular disease state or some other physiological state of an organism. (source: Wikipedia)

Benign Prostate Hyperplasia (BPH): Enlargement of the prostate gland unrelated to prostate cancer. Also called BPH. BPH can have similar symptoms to prostate cancer, but is not cancerous, and often occurs because of the prostate's natural tendency to get bigger with age.

Brachytherapy (seeds): Implanting radioactive "seeds" or minute chunks of radioactive material, into the prostate to kill cancer.

Cancer: Unregulated or abnormal cell growth. Cancerous cells build up to form a tumor, which can then spread to other parts of the body.

Caregiver: Someone who provides support and care to an individual struggling with a debilitating condition. Caregivers can provide many different types of support, from driving another individual to their doctor's appointments, helping with chores, and much more. Caregivers can also be prone to depression and burnout if they do not have adequate support from others.

Castration or Orchiectomy: The surgical removal of the testicles. Can be performed on one or both testicles. Often used as a method of hormone therapy since it essentially stops testosterone production. If both testicles are removed it's called surgical castration.

Catheter : See Foley Catheter and/or Supra Pubic Catheter

Chemotherapy: The treatment of disease by the use of chemical substances, especially the treatment of cancer by cytotoxic and other drugs.

Comorbidity: Two or more conditions occurring at the same time. For example, if an individual has diabetes and prostate cancer, both conditions are considered comorbidities in that individual. Comorbidities can result from independent factors or can develop as a result of one another or a common factor.

Cojones: Spanish for Testicles

Depends: (noun) adult diaper or (verb) standard response to "How are you doing after daVinci surgery?"

Dysuria: painful or difficult urination.

Ejaculation: Emission of semen at the climax of intercourse.

Erectile Dysfunction: The inability to have an erection sufficient for intercourse.

Foley Catheter: A catheter inserted into the penis and threaded through the urethra into the bladder, where it is anchored in place with a tiny, inflated balloon. It removes urine from the body.

Four-K (4K score): The 4Kscore Test helps clarify the biopsy decision-making process by determining a patient specific probability for finding aggressive, Gleason score 7 or higher prostate cancer upon biopsy.

FUBAR - Term originated in the armed forces during WWII. An acronym for Fucked Up Beyond All Repair

General Anesthesia: is a combination of medications that put you in a sleep-like state before a surgery or other medical procedure. Under general anesthesia, you don't feel pain because you're completely unconscious. General anesthesia usually uses a combination of intravenous drugs and inhaled gasses (anesthetics)

Gleason: (to combat your prostate cancer with old-school humor as in Jackie Gleason in The Honeymooners).

Gleason score: Used to assess the aggressiveness or predicted path of an individual's prostate cancer. Lower Gleason scores represent less aggressive cancers while higher scores are more aggressive. An individual's Gleason score can be between 2 and 10, and is the result of the two most common cancer cell types present, with the most common of the two cell types listed first. An example Gleason score could be 3+4=7 or 4+3=7, with the second score being slightly more aggressive than the first since the primary tumor cell type is a 4 rather than a 3.

Hernia: Inguinal hernias are the most common type of hernia. ... These hernias occur when the intestines push through a weak spot or tear in the lower abdominal wall, often in the inguinal canal. The inguinal canal is found in your groin. In men, it's the area where the spermatic cord passes from the abdomen to the scrotum.

Hormone Therapy: Also called ADT for Androgen deprivation therapy: the use of hormones to treat advanced prostate cancer.It is aimed at shutting down the hormones that nourish the prostate.

Kegels: Kegel exercises for men can strengthen the pelvic floor muscles, which support the bladder and bowel and affect sexual function. With practice, Kegel exercises for men can be done just about anytime.Before you start doing Kegel exercises, find out how to locate the correct muscles and understand the proper technique.

Immunotherapy: treatment designed to maximize the immune system's ability to fight cancer

Laparoscopy: a surgical procedure in which a fiber-optic instrument is inserted through the abdominal wall to view the organs in the abdomen or to permit a surgical procedure.

Lymph Nodes: are small, round structures that play a vital role in the body's immune system.

Mad - On : An attitude which is portrayed by a person who is perceived to dislike everyone and therefore appears mad.

Male sling: The male sling procedure helps men with urinary incontinence due to sphincter weakness or insufficiency caused by prior pelvic surgery including TURP (transurthethral resection of the prostate) and radical prostatectomy. In the male sling procedure, synthetic mesh-like tape is positioned around part of the urethral bulb, slightly compressing the urethra and moving it into a new position -- overcoming the problem of urinary incontinence in many patients.

Malignant: A term used to describe aggressive cancers with high potential of invading other areas of the body.

Metastasis: When a malignant cancer spreads beyond its initial site to invade other parts of the body. The cancer may spread beyond the prostate into nearby structures, lymph nodes, or spread to distant organs or the bone

Morbidity: Refers to having a disease or a symptom of disease, or to the amount of disease within a population. Morbidity also refers to medical problems caused by a treatment.

Neoplasm: Abnormal growths of tissue that are also referred to as tumors. Neoplasms can be cancerous or non-cancerous (benign).See tumor

Oncologist: A physician who is specially trained to diagnose and treat cancer.

Overflow incontinence:s a form of urinary incontinence, characterized by the involuntary release of urine from an overfull urinary bladder, often in the absence of any urge to urinate.

Palliative Care: Medical care that focuses on making a struggling individual comfortable. Relies on a team approach of many physicians, counselors, health aides, and more, to provide support to both the individual and their family. Palliative care does not need to be related to in-home care or end-of-life care; it can be provided to an individual during any phase of their treatment, but these are common examples of when it is utilized (similar to Hospice care)

Pelvic floor muscle: The pelvic floor muscles support the contents of the pelvis. The pelvic floor or pelvic diaphragm is composed of muscle fibers of the levator ani, the coccygeus muscle, and associated connective tissue which span the area underneath the pelvis

Perineum: the area between the anus and the scrotum. You don't want to go there.

Primary/adjuvant therapy: Primary therapy is the main treatment used for a condition, while an adjuvant therapy is added onto the primary treatment to either provide further support, address other symptoms, increase the effectiveness of the primary treatment, or prevent the cancer from coming back.

Prostate Gland: Gland located between the bladder and the base of the penis that secretes a fluid that will eventually become a part of semen. The prostate gland is part of the male reproductive system and functions to produce fluid to nourish and protect sperm cells

Prostate Specific Antigen (PSA) Test: A common initial screening method for prostate cancer. Measures the amount of prostate-specific antigen in the blood. Typically, higher PSA levels are seen in individuals with prostate cancer.

PSA level: Number of nanograms of PSA per milliliter (ng/ml) of blood

PSA density: The PSA level in comparison to the size of the prostate. It is calculated by dividing the PSA level by the size of the prostate (as measured by transrectal ultrasound-TRUS)

PSA velocity: Measure of how much PSA levels change within a given period of time

PSA Doubling time: The amount of time it takes for the PSA level to double

Radiation therapy: A curative treatment for prostate cancer. It involves beaming X-ray energy into a prostate tumor from the outside for a few minutes at a time over the course of a several weeks.

Robot Assisted Radical Prostatectomy (da Vinci): The da Vinci surgical system is a robotic surgical system made by the American company Intuitive Surgical. Approved by the Food and Drug Administration in 2000, it is designed to facilitate complex surgery using a minimally invasive approach, and is controlled by a surgeon from a console. (source: Wikipedia)

Salvage Therapy: A medical term for "Plan B". It is another form of treatment given because the first form of treatment he patient underwent wasn't successful in curing the problem. In prostate cancer, this mainly the use of radiation therapy, cryoablation therapy, or hormonal therapy.

Seeds: See Brachytherapy or Radiation Therapy.

Seminal Vesicles: Each of a pair of glands which open into the vas deferens near to its junction with the urethra and secrete many of the components of semen.

Stress incontinence: is the unintentional loss of urine. Stress incontinence happens when physical movement or activity — such as coughing, sneezing, running or heavy lifting — puts pressure (stress) on your bladder

Suprapubic Catheter: is a type of urinary catheter. It empties the bladder through an incision in the belly instead of a tube in the urethra.

Testosterone: Testosterone is the primary male sex hormone and an anabolic steroid. In male humans, testosterone plays a key role in the development of male reproductive tissues such as testes and prostate, as well as promoting secondary sexual characteristics such as increased muscle and bone mass, and the growth of body hair. (source: Wikipedia)

Testosterone Replacement Therapy (TRT): Androgen replacement therapy, often referred to as testosterone replacement therapy, is a form of hormone therapy in which androgens, often testosterone, are replaced. ART is often prescribed to counter the effects of male hypogonadism. (source: Wikipedia)

Tumor: A tumor, also known as a neoplasm, is an abnormal mass of tissue that may be solid or fluid-filled. ... Malignant: Malignant tumors are cancerous. ... Some benign tumors can eventually become premalignant, and then malignant.

Urethra: is a tube that connects the urinary bladder to the urinary meatus for the removal of urine from the body. In males, the urethra travels through the penis and also carries semen.

Urge incontinence: Occurs when you have a sudden urge to urinate. In urge incontinence, the bladder contracts when it shouldn't, causing some urine to leak through the sphincter muscles holding the bladder closed. Other names for this condition are: overactive bladder. bladder spasms.

Urinary incontinence: Is the involuntary leakage of urine. It means a person urinates when they do not want to. Control over the urinary sphincter is either lost or weakened.

Urology: Also known as genitourinary surgery, is the branch of medicine that focuses on surgical and medical diseases of the male and female urinary-tract system and the male reproductive organs. (source: Wikipedia)

Vas deferens: the vas deferens transports mature sperm to the urethra, the tube that carries urine or sperm to outside of the body, in preparation for ejaculation. Ejaculatory ducts: These are formed by the fusion of the vas deferens and the seminal vesicles

Watchful Waiting: Is an approach to a medical problem in which time is allowed to pass before medical intervention or therapy is used. During this time, repeated testing may be performed. Related terms include expectant management, active surveillance and masterly inactivity.

Book Review

Guide to Surviving Prostate Cancer
Patrick C. Walsh, MD and Janet Farrar Worthington
Hachette Book Group
Fourth Edition, Revised and Updated May 2018
Amazon: $13.99 Soft Cover (Also available on Kindle and Hardcover)

(Author note: this review originally appeared in February, 2019 on www.prostate.net)

There are over 9,000 books on Amazon discussing prostate cancer. The National Institutes for Health, and many cancer websites, are loaded with useful updated information on prostate cancer and therapies. But like trying to take a sip from the proverbial fire hose, where do you focus when the cancer happening to you?

In May of 2018, I was diagnosed with T1C prostate cancer with a Gleason score of 7 (4+3). An MRI the following month confirmed the biopsy visually An MRI the following month confirmed the the biopsy results. Early detection confirmed complete containment with my prostate gland. The cancer hadn't spread, but it might have if I ignored it. Fortunately, my neighbor Tom Knox shared Dr. Patrick Walsh's book with me. Tom is a prostate cancer survivor too.

My wife and I studied it cover to cover the week before I met with my urologist, all 524 pages of it. Armed with questions we were prepared to discuss every treatment option.

In the revised and updated Fourth Edition, Walsh covers the what, why, and how of prostate cancer and therapies, supported by years of data. For the new version, Walsh relies on leading experts in the diagnosis and treatment of prostate cancer, as well as specialists in Oncology, ED treatment, active surveillance, and epidemiology. The original illustrations done by the late Leon Schlossberg leave nothing to the imagination.

What makes this book better than all of the rest in my estimation is that it's the complete current guide to prostate cancer, supported by decades of data or facts. It's written for the prostate cancer patient and advocate.

Dr. Walsh is a leading (and legendary) surgeon and one of the most respected prostate disease specialist in the world. He's the surgeon who developed a nerve sparing procedure which is very important to having erections following radical surgery.

Each chapter starts with and a highly abridged version of its contents, a CliffsNotes for us speed readers. Chapter one focuses on the prostate and there's a crash course to get you up to speed quickly on the walnut shaped capsule located below your bladder.

All the treatment options available have life-changing impact, but in fact, they suck. There are three primary goals in surviving prostate cancer: 1) Reduce or eliminate the cancer, 2) Quality of daily life ie. incontinence, and 3) sexual functionality (ED).

Dr. Walsh debunks the 2012 recommendation by the U.S. Preventative Service Task force against routine screening for prostate cancer. They did so without the guidance of one urologist. Government in action.

Unfortunately, thousands of men have been diagnosed with prostate cancer but were told by their family doctor they didn't need to be screened. Even today I have friends who have family doctors with that philosophy. Even today! Incredible. In addition it has been found that Afro Americans have a higher risk than of prostate cancer than Caucasians and for years they have been treated based upon the same data.

Remember, you are here to find the truth and make educated decisions based upon proven facts. Dr. Walsh and his partner in writing this book Janet Farrar Worthington don't mince words. They don't try to convince you of one treatment option or another. They speak the truth and arm you for your journey of discovery with your urologist, oncologist, or surgeon. *Guide to Survive Prostate Cancer* should anchor your library of information on prostate cancer.

Contributors

Richard Bevan-Thomas, MD

Rich Bevan-Thomas graduated from Duke University and subsequently completed his masters in anatomy and his medical degree at St. Louis University School of Medicine. He completed his general surgery internship and urologic surgery residency at the University of Texas Houston Health Science Center and MD Anderson Cancer Center. After completing his residency, he joined East Bay Urology in San Ramon, California. This is where Dr. Bevan-Thomas specialized in minimally invasive procedures, laparoscopic and robotic surgery utilizing the daVinci® surgical system.

In 2007, Dr. Bevan-Thomas was invited to join UANT as part of the one of the world's largest robotic surgery programs. He has an extensive experience with robotic surgery and began performing robotic surgery in 2002. Since then, he has worked as a consultant for Intuitive Surgical assisting with education and video presentations.

Dr. Bevan-Thomas' recognitions include the Pfizer scholar in Urology and the Gerald G. Murphy scholar in Urology in 2002. He was the previous chief of Surgery at San Ramon Regional Medical Center prior to joining UANT in 2007. He has been a proctor and instructor in the field of robotics since 2003 and continues to take in interest in patient and physician education.

He also works in educating other surgeons as a proctor in the field of cryosurgery with both prostate and kidney cryoablation. He is currently a member of the American Urological Association, Texas Urologic Society, The Society of Laparoendoscopic Surgeons, and Tarrant County Medical Society.

Dr. Bevan-Thomas and his wife and 3 children live the Dallas metroplex and they are ecstatic to be back in Texas. He enjoys Karate where he has served as a black belt instructor in several different styles and continues to train and compete in the Martial Arts.

Robert "Bob" Tierno

Bob Tierno has been around the block, and the cell-block.

In his storied career (and there are many stories), he has been a correctional officer, federal prison systems regional manager, Intel automotive marketing manager field sales engineer, district sales manager, a Bed & Breakfast owner in the Gold Country foothills of the California Sierras, a franchise business coach and a semi-retired consultant.

What ties it all together for Bob is the knack for leading business growth strategies and then executing on them, relentlessly.

He enjoys the gift of quickly learning the intricacies of diverse industries. Never one to rest in the comfort zone of a silo, he is experienced in sales, marketing, business development, and operations.

Bob holds an MBA from Pepperdine University and a BS in History from the University of Oklahoma. He served as a Captain in the U.S. Army Reserves from 1972-1986.

He has always been passionate about communication, integrity and leadership, and with this book, he is now adding the title of Author to his resume.

Printed in Great Britain
by Amazon